THE WISDOM OF THE FOREST UNLOCKED

Uncover Hidden Intelligence, Gain Rare Insight, Grow Resilient, and Delve into the Secrets of Woodland's Whispers

by

DR. MANOJ SARKAR

Email: manojkumarsarkar1954@gmail.com

Website: https://niveditatrichy.org

DEDICATED TO

All the noble souls who served in the past, and who are serving now selflessly for the Protection, Conservation, and Augmentation of the Plants, and their home - the Forests- the Ecosystem of our survival on this beautiful planet -the Earth.

ACKNOWLEDGEMENTS

I am indebted to Dr. Aruna Basu Sarcar IFS (Rtd.) for her continuous encouragement to continue my writing by providing me with all kinds of services and support during this journey...

My humble gratitude to **Mr. Som Bathla**, who is an Amazon #1 **Bestselling author** of multiple books; for mentoring, motivating, and guiding me to **Write, Self-Publish, & Launch Books** and for helping me start my Authorpreneur Journey.

I am thankful to Mr. Ravi Tewari and Mr. Sooraj Achar who is also Amazon's #1 **Bestselling authors** of multiple books for their help in publishing this book.

I am grateful to author Dr. Sapna Deb for her guidance in writing this book.

WE INVOKE THIS BOOK

Let us invoke this book with a verse composed and sung by Michael Tierra* about the unleashed wisdom, and encouraging and creative healing energy being rendered since time immemorial by the Forests- the home of the Plant Community all over the planet to all living beings including the Humanity as:

"To all green, growing, flowering ones of this

beautiful planet,

who embody the universal creative healing

energy,

and with each moment,

humbly assume the ground task of transforming

light into life,

and who patiently bear the crude assaults and

inserts of our misguided ignorance,

all in the dream of awakening,

Without their conscious, living presence,

Nothing, no breath no food,

no life,

no delight,

None of our earthly endeavors would be possible"

** Michael Tierra*

"I salute this selfless living Kingdom of Plants with all my humility & take these endeavors in conserving, protecting & propagating them to receive their unleashed wisdom and auspicious healing energy for all of this planet- the Mother Earth."

- Manoj sarkar

*Michael Tierra is a pioneer in the study of traditional Chinese and Ayurvedic medicine in the West. He is one of the forerunners of the North American Natural Health movement.

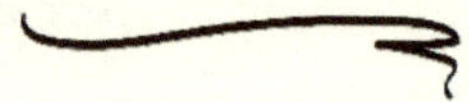

AN APPEAL

(TO ALL MEMBERS OF HUMANITY)

Dear Friends,

Every fraction of a minute you, me, and all other living beings on this planet- the Earth, inhale oxygen of which 98% comes from plants and 80% of our food gets from plants. The entire day and night, 24 hours and 7 days a week in our lifetime we survived because of the benevolent Services of these Plants and their habitat- the Forests.

Thanks to the pioneering work demonstrated by Jagadish Chandra Bose at the Royal Society in London, England in 1901. Sir J.C. Bose proved that plants are like any other **life form.** They have a definite life cycle, and a reproductive system, and are sensitive to **pain and affection like humans**.

Now we understand that plants are sentient beings, capable of feeling and awareness. Just as we need oxygen to survive, we must recognize the crucial role of plants in sustaining life on Earth.

Friends,

We can survive for a few days without food and water, but can we survive even for a few minutes without oxygen? Have you given a thought to this life form of plants which is our lifeline?

If not, I urge you to connect with plants on a deeper level, acknowledging their importance and asking how we can serve them. This intuitive connection can guide us towards **selflessness and positive action, fostering a deeper respect for all living beings.**

I have experienced and documented this in my first book ***"Self-Mastery & Enlightenment through the Kingdom of Plants"***

Let us reflect on the critical role of plants during the **COVID-19 pandemic when the struggle for oxygen** underscored our dependence on nature. By cultivating empathy and reverence for plants, we can combat deforestation and mitigate the effects of climate change.

Your mere feeling for the plants, will not allow you to tear or cut any plant anymore and you will get **true affection and more positive thoughts** for them.

If all of us together follow this as the Japanese and the Bhutanese respect and love the plants, there will not be any climate change, global warming, cloud bursting, floods, and drought.

In such a situation our affected Earth would be protected from deforestation in the universe, of course, **we must stop wars among countries and stop the genocide of humanity by damaging the ever-green plants and forests.**

Yours sincerely

MS

WHY IS THIS BOOK UNIQUE FOR YOU?

The book *"The Wisdom of the Forest Unlocked,"* promises an intriguing exploration into the hidden realms of nature and the profound lessons waiting to be discovered within forests.

It delves into how plants (flora) play a critical role in sustaining life on Earth, providing oxygen and food for all living beings (fauna) including humanity. How the plants communicate, adapt, and thrive through interconnected systems, offering their **Contribution, Special qualities, and the Secret life** applicable to human life and society.

This book illustrates prime facts through charts, figures, maps, photographs, and tables for easy understanding by the readers.

It referred to the pioneering work of Jagadish Chandra Bose, who proved that plants are like any other **life form and are sensitive to pain and affection** in 1901 at the Royal Society in London, England.

The book takes readers on a journey into the mystical 'whispers' of the woods—**revealing the secrets of biodiversity worldwide through various forest types their regeneration, threats, and symbiosis.** It encourages readers to attune their senses to nature's **subtle voice** - the concept of **biophilia**, as popularized by biologist E.O. Wilson.

"The Wisdom of the Forest Unlocked" serves as a call to action in discovering the **actual causes of deforestation, its effects, and a plan for its strategic control.**

It emphasizes and highlights the value of simplicity, patience, and interconnectedness as learned from **centuries of tragic forest evolution.**

Finally, the book promises a captivating exploration of the forest's wisdom—unveiling its hidden intelligence, offering practical recommendations that humanity must have active and dynamic wisdom to address the unheard cry of plants and forests - the lifeline of all living beings on the planet Earth.

In conclusion, the author appeals for collective action to protect plants and the planet, envisioning a harmonious future where humans respect their counterpart- the Kingdom Plantae and protect, preserve, and promote the natural world in perpetuity.

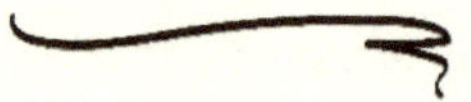

TABLE OF CONTENTS

INTRODUCTION

The Wisdom of the Plants and the Forests

Wisdom! Let us see what this word carries for humans and the Forests.

It is a store of knowledge in action that gives Jivanmukta to an individual. (that is freedom in a lifetime). **A Jivanmukta,** literally meaning **'liberated while living'**, is a person who, in Vedanta philosophy has gained complete self-knowledge.

How is Jivanmukta connected with the plants and forest?

Truly speaking, every plant is in a Jivanmukta state having no fear, no selfishness, no genocide but **they give everything to others and take the position of a Giver,** unlike humans who like to do everything for themselves or their family except a group of people who are aligned with spirituality.

As plants are always in the Jivanmukta state maybe because of this, **Gautam Buddha** took shelter for his meditation below a Jivanmukta tree that is the *Ficus religiosa* (Pipal tree).

Maybe For the same reason even in Sacred literature like the **Bhagavad Gita** --the Lord Krishna mentioned in Vibhuti yoga (10.26) that among the trees **"I am the Asvattha"** - the *Ficus religiosa* (Pipal tree). Each tree is a symbol of the Jivanmukta state and they continue to give lessons of **Tyaga or the Sacrifice.**

The forest is a home for all the Jivanmukta plants, each of them takes the help of each other and makes goodwill feelings for all the other living beings unlike the human and other animal kingdoms.

The basic difference between humans and plants is that the man wants everything for himself or his family members while the **Plants or their home-- the Forest gives everything to others.** This is the quality - **the WISDOM** that we humans must learn from the Plants and Forests, love each other, stop genocide, and **protect these noble living organisms the plants and forests for our posterity.**

Before the advent of the 20th century, science did not acknowledge the vitality of trees and plants. Then, on **May 10, 1901, Jagadish Chandra Bose proved that plants are like any other life form.**

Sir J.C. Bose proved that plants have a definite life cycle, and a reproductive system and are aware of their surroundings. The demonstration took place at the Royal Society in London, England.

Bose was the first to study the action of microwaves in plant tissues and the changes in the plant cell membrane potential. Through this study, he proved that **plants are sensitive to pain and affection'**

The Plants are the only living entity that sacrifices everything for the benefit of others including mankind. Forests - the home of the Plants work as a storehouse to supply all the Basic Life Supporting Systems (BLSS). Besides, the tangible and intangible flow of benefits, the Kingdom of Plants also extends subtle blessings and wisdom to the aspirants through their spirit of unending services in silence as Monks. Thus, forests as a composition of innumerable plants operate as the 'Sea of Monks' being the panacea to human beings and other living organisms.

These very facts urge for a committed, logical, and scientific approach to protect, conserve, manage, and expand our forest resources for the present as well as for the generations to come.

The concept of the "Wisdom of the Forests" refers to the collective intelligence and interconnectedness of forest ecosystems. By recognizing and honoring the wisdom inherent in forests, we can cultivate a deeper appreciation for the interconnected web of life and work towards a more sustainable and harmonious future for all beings. Some of the salient features of the wisdom of forests are elaborated below:

1. **Interconnectedness and Balance:** Forests are complex ecosystems where various species of plants, animals, fungi, and microorganisms interact in intricate ways. The interconnectedness of these components forms a delicate balance that sustains the health and vitality of the forest as a whole.

2. **Adaptability and Resilience:** Forests have evolved over millions of years, developing strategies for adaptation and resilience in the face of environmental challenges. They demonstrate the wisdom of flexibility, resilience, and the ability to thrive amidst change, offering valuable lessons for human societies in navigating uncertainties and challenges.

3. **Sustainability and Regeneration:** Forests operate on principles of sustainability and regeneration, where resources are utilized efficiently, and waste is minimized. They teach us the importance of living in harmony with nature, practicing stewardship, and ensuring that our actions support the long-term health and vitality of ecosystems for future generations.

4. **Diversity and Collaboration:** Forests thrive on diversity, with a multitude of species coexisting and collaborating within the ecosystem. Forests are biodiversity hotspots, harboring a rich variety of plant and animal species. This biodiversity contributes to the overall health and stability of the ecosystem, promoting resilience and resistance to disease and pests.

5. **Cyclical Patterns and Seasons:** Forests operate in cyclical patterns, following the rhythms of the seasons and natural cycles of growth, decay, and regeneration. They teach us about the importance of honoring these natural rhythms, living in harmony with the cycles of life, and embracing the wisdom of patience, renewal, and transformation.

6. **Interdependence and Mutual Support:** Within forests, organisms depend on each other for survival, forming intricate webs of mutual support and cooperation. The wisdom of the forests reminds us of the importance of cultivating relationships based on mutual respect, empathy, and support in human societies as well as with the plant communities recognizing that we are all interconnected and interdependent.

7. **Sustainability and Stewardship:** Forests provide a multitude of ecological, economic, and cultural benefits to humans, including clean air and water, carbon sequestration, timber and non-timber forest products, and recreational opportunities. However, these benefits are contingent upon responsible stewardship and sustainable management practices.

8. **Timelessness and Wisdom:** Forests are ancient and enduring ecosystems that have stood the test of time. They carry within them a wealth of knowledge and wisdom accumulated over millennia of evolution and adaptation. By spending time in forests and immersing

ourselves in their natural rhythms and cycles, we can tap into this timeless wisdom and gain a deeper understanding of our place in the world.

Overall, this Introduction advocates for recognizing and respecting the wisdom inherent in forests, which can deepen our appreciation for the interconnected web of life and guide efforts toward a more sustainable future for present humanity and plants and forests and their progeny to come.

PART - I: FORESTS - THE HOME OF PLANTS AND THEIR CONTRIBUTION TO HUMANITY

Chapter 1: The Forests created living Homes for Humans and all living beings, provided food, Air, and Water...

"FORESTS" - A Storehouse for Supplying the Basic Life Supporting Systems to all the living beings of this planet- the Earth".

We are in the Kingdom of Plants which includes all flora, from minuscule mosses to massive trees. Our lives depend on plants - we must value their contributions, and we must acknowledge, appreciate, and take all measures to protect and propagate them for our survival.

The research Proceedings of the National Academy of Sciences USA observes that with over 4,00,000 known species, they account for 80% of total biomass or lifeforms on Earth. Bacteria stand second with only 15%, whereas we humans cover 0.01%.

Land plants first appeared 500 million years ago on Earth with trees emerging 370 million years ago. As the number of plants increased, they removed more and more carbon dioxide from the atmosphere, cooling Earth and emitting oxygen, enabling mankind and other animals.

It was the majestic science of plants their photosynthesis turns water, sunlight, and carbon dioxide into oxygen and sugars—that made human life possible through the gifts of air and food.

The kingdom of plants Humanity has 80% of the food we eat and 98% of the oxygen we inhale.

The extraordinary kingdom of plants is now under siege. The State of the World's Plants and Fungi Report finds that 40 % of these species face different degrees of threats including even their extinction.

The plant species are confronting the large-scale destruction of habitat for commercial farming, livestock rearing, and construction in the name of development. Plants are embattled by climate change, caused by anthropogenic emissions alerting Earth's air, water, and heat triggering floods, droughts fires, and pestilence.

The Food and Agriculture (FAO) finds that 40% of all crops are already lost annually, leaving millions facing hunger.

For the survival of man, he needs food to eat, air to breathe water to drink, and lifesaving drugs at the time of his ailments. All these requirements form the Basic Life Supporting System for human beings. Forests, work as a storehouse for supplying all these Basic life-supporting systems to mankind including other animals and Micro creatures.

In the conventional system of valuation of forests mainly the benefits flow of tangible parameters was calculated. All existing public policies are mostly limited within the benefit flows mainly fuel, fodder, timber, etc., while the importance of Forests has to be evaluated more deeply for the posterity of the entire living being.

Hence, the existing policies both at the local, state, and national levels for every country need to be looked into more carefully, especially in

- Policies related to the felling of trees.

- Total protection and conservation-oriented controlling system.

- An inventory to be carried out for all plant resources of all Districts / Forest Division (as a unit of the entire country).

- Soon after inventory the Biochemical test, and quantity of various alkaloids, etc., are to be made for finalizing the suitability of the plants.

- Special attention is to be taken for making an inventory of all plants that suffer from various degrees of threats and comprehensive action is to be prepared to ensure their identification, protection, conservation, and propagation at the earliest.

i) Special role of Oxygen, and Shares of Other Gases Flow in the Atmosphere.

Gases	Symbols	Content in %
Nitrogen	N_2	78.084%
Oxygen	O_2	20.947%
Argon	Ar	0.934%
Carbon dioxide	CO_2	0.035%

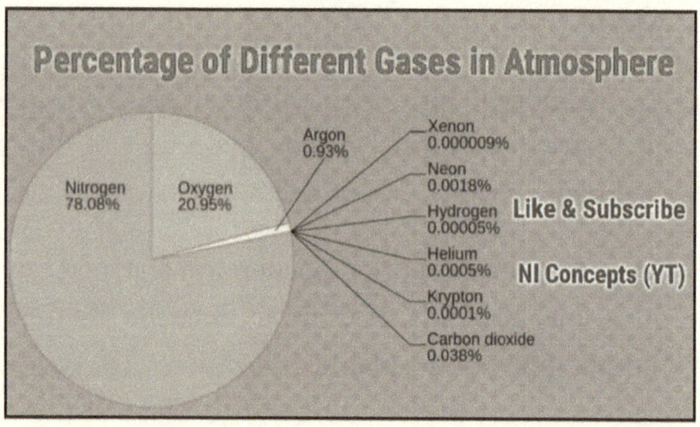

All of Earth's oxygen does not come from trees alone. Rather, the atmospheric oxygen that we depend on as humans comes predominantly from the ocean. According to National Geographic, about 70% of the oxygen in the atmosphere comes from marine plants and plant-like organisms.

These ocean-living plants release molecular oxygen as a waste product of photosynthesis (as do most plants). In photosynthesis, plants capture sunlight and use its energy to split carbon dioxide and water, making sugar for itself and releasing oxygen as a by-product.

The dominance of ocean life as Earth's top oxygen producer makes sense when you consider that the majority of the Earth is covered with ocean.

Phytoplankton is the dominant class of the different types of marine life providing oxygen. Phytoplankton are microscopic photosynthesizing organisms that live in water. Phytoplankton includes cyanobacteria, green algae, diatoms, and dinoflagellates.

Although too small to be visible to the human eye by itself, when many phytoplankton clump together they look like green ocean slime. The oxygen we depend on from breath to breath is provided mostly by a vast army of invisible sea creatures.

No more, it is a myth that there will not be any required O2 flow in the atmosphere if there is no plant on the Earth's surface. No plants – No creation of O2 in the atmosphere & hence no breathing is possible for mankind & other animal kingdoms.

Further, the terrestrial Plants - namely Trees, shrubs, herbs, grass, liana, climbers, etc., are the O2-producing factories. Forests as the home of such trees, shrubs, Herbs, etc., are gigantic O2-producing factories blessed by nature for the survival of human beings.

However, we humans still claim, provoke, and recommend the diversion of forestlands for non-forestry purposes and tree felling – in the name of so-called development!

Every citizen of this planet needs to live with good health and prosperity, not at the cost of any other living beings particularly those who help us in our daily lives with basic life-supporting systems like Food, Water, and Air. The plants and their habitats- the forests provide us with all these prime resources for humans and also other living beings. ***So, we do not and should not exploit or destroy this living species like us- the plants in the name of development. We love them and protect them creating awareness among all sections of humanities.***

ii) Water Supply:

We get water from rain, from the subsoil, or the flowing water like rivers or lakes. Truly speaking the basic source of freshwater- is precipitation either in the form of raindrops or in the form of snowfall.

India is a fortunate country to have sufficient rainfall for a span of 4 to 5 months from South West and North East monsoon. Even in some places, the rainfall is more than 8 months. However, unfortunately, without having a sufficient storage system, *in-situ* infiltration in the subsoil usually could not happen in our country. Hence, almost more than 80% of such rainwater reaches to Bay of Bengal / Arabian Sea as surface runoff immediately after the rainfall.

Similar situations are prevalent in many other developing countries without having sufficient soil and moisture conservation measures.

Hence, to top this surface runoff we have to enhance the Forest cover all over the country irrespective of the legal status of the land. At least 33% of the land needs to be covered with trees, shrubs, and herbs, if possible, with 3 to 4-tires forest canopy cover. This helps in dispersing each raindrop into minute particles and allows percolate slowly in the subsoil enhancing the groundwater discharge and stopping the surface off.

iii) Source of Fertile Soils

For producing food crops, we need fertile loamy soil which is mainly a mixture of humus colloids that comes mainly from plants or largely from Forests. Mechanical use of chemical fertilizers proved to be fatal to destroy soil health. Hence, Healthy fertile soil that is the product of the Forest has a direct role in public life in producing food crops – using natural and fertile soils. The application of chemical fertilizers needs to be reduced and there needs to be policy decisions.

iv) Medicinal Plants for Life-Saving Drugs

After finding out the list of plants with Medicinal properties – the plants with lifesaving drugs are to be separated. Their Zone of Endemism maps can be prepared and special care may be given to such plants both for their protection, conservation, and further propagation and for patenting such plants of rare availability for preparing lifesaving drugs.

Finally, Public Policy for the protection of existing forests and forestland, increasing the forest cover of the country essentially needs to be framed. Further, protecting the fragile Ecosystem – restoring fresh O2 flow, promoting perennial water flow – protecting the natural water bodies, enhancing groundwater discharge raising ground water table, and ensuring sustained yield of life-saving drugs from the forest are required to be outlined in Public Policy for all countries.

Chapter 1: Key Takeaways

1. The page emphasizes the critical contributions of plants and forests to sustaining life on Earth, highlighting their role in providing oxygen, food, water, and life-saving drugs. It discusses the threats facing plant species and forests due to habitat destruction, climate change, and unsustainable practices.

2. Key points include the importance of forests as oxygen-producing factories, the necessity of forest conservation for water management, the role of forests in maintaining fertile soils, and the urgency of public policy interventions to safeguard ecosystems and promote sustainable living.

Overall, the article calls for urgent action to safeguard forests and their invaluable contributions to sustaining life on Earth.

Chapter 2: The Plants and their home – the Forests -the Ecosystem of our life

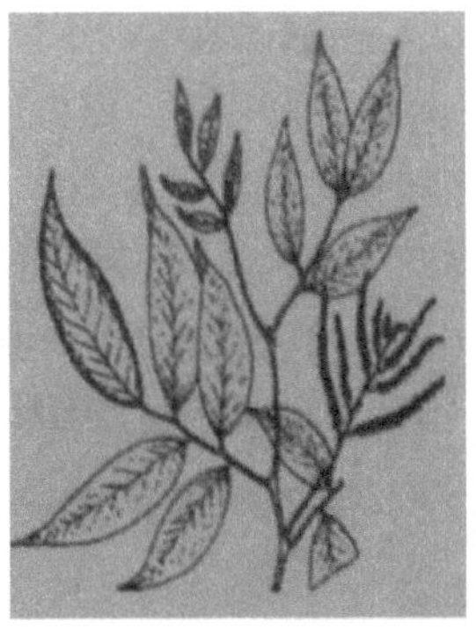

The Kingdom of Plants includes all flora, from minuscule mosses to massive trees on the terrestrial land and the microscopic phytoplankton of various types to the seagrasses in the sea.

Trees, shrubs, herbs, grasses, liana, climbers, stragglers, orchids, etc form the plants from the terrestrial landmass in Forests. At the same time, marine plants and plant-like organisms like Phytoplankton live in water. Phytoplankton are microscopic photosynthesizing organisms that include cyanobacteria, green algae, diatoms, dinoflagellates, etc. Although too small to be visible to the human eye by itself, when many phytoplankton clump together they look like green ocean slime.

Both the plants from the land and the sea together produce 98% of the oxygen we inhale and 80% of the food we eat. According to National Geographic, about 70% of the oxygen in the atmosphere comes from marine plants and plant-like organisms.

Forest definitions, and comparisons to other datasets and their utilities:

There is no universal definition of what a 'forest' is. That means there are a range of estimates of forest area, and how this has changed over time. The UN FAO has a very specific definition of a forest. It's "land spanning more than 0.5 hectares with trees higher than 0.5 meters and a canopy cover of more than 10%, or trees able to reach these thresholds in situ."

In other words, it has criteria for the area that must be covered (0.5 hectares), the minimum height of trees (0.5 meters), and a density of at least 10%.

Compare this to the UN Framework on Climate Change (UNFCCC), which uses forest estimates to calculate land use carbon emissions, and for its REDD+ program, where low-to-middle-income countries can receive finance for verified projects that prevent or reduce deforestation. It defines a forest as having a density of 10-30%, a minimum tree height of 2-5 meters, and a smaller area of 0.1 hectares.

It's not just forest definitions that vary between sources. Global Forest Watch is an interactive online dashboard that tracks 'tree loss' and 'forest losses across the world. It measures this in real time and can provide better estimates of year-to-year variations in rates of tree loss. However, the UN FAO and Global Forest Watch do not measure the same thing.

The UN FAO measures deforestation based on how land is used. It measures the permanent conversion of forested land to another use, such as pasture, croplands, or urbanization.

Global Forest Watch (GFW) measures temporary changes in forests. It can detect changes in land cover but does not differentiate the underlying land use.

As GFW describes in its definition of 'forest loss': "Loss" indicates the removal or mortality of tree cover and can be due to a variety of factors, including mechanical harvesting, fire, disease, or storm damage. As such, "loss" does not equate to deforestation."

Since GFW uses satellite imagery, its methods continually improve. This makes its ability to detect changes in forest cover even stronger.

What data from GFW makes clear is that forest loss across the tropics is still very high, and in the last few years, little progress has been made. Since UN FAO reports are only published in 5-year intervals, they miss these shorter-term fluctuations in forest loss. The GFW's shorter-interval stocktakes of how countries are doing will become increasingly valuable.

Forests are extensive areas covered chiefly with trees and undergrowth. Forests play crucial roles in maintaining ecological balance, supporting biodiversity, regulating climate, providing habitats for various organisms, and offering resources and ecosystem services vital for human well-being.

Forest types are broadly categorized into tropical rainforests, temperate forests, boreal forests, and deciduous forests, among others, (Vide chapter-III for more details).

Furthermore, forests provide resources such as timber, food, medicine, and fuelwood, and they offer recreational and spiritual value to communities worldwide. Overall, forests are complex ecosystems that contribute significantly to both ecological and human well-being.

Chapter 2: Key Takeaways

1. The note discusses the significance of plants and forests in the ecosystem of life, highlighting their diversity and vital role in providing oxygen and food. It explores various definitions of forests and the differences in forest measurements used by organizations like the UN FAO and Global Forest Watch.

2. It emphasizes the ongoing challenges of forest loss, particularly in tropical regions, and the importance of real-time monitoring. It concludes by underscoring the cultural, social, and economic importance of forests to communities worldwide.

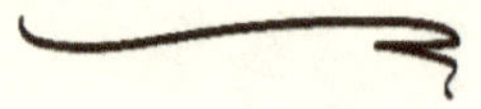

PART -II: THE RARE QUALITIES OF PLANTS AND THEIR SECRET LIFE

Chapter 3: The Rare Qualities of Plants, and Forests

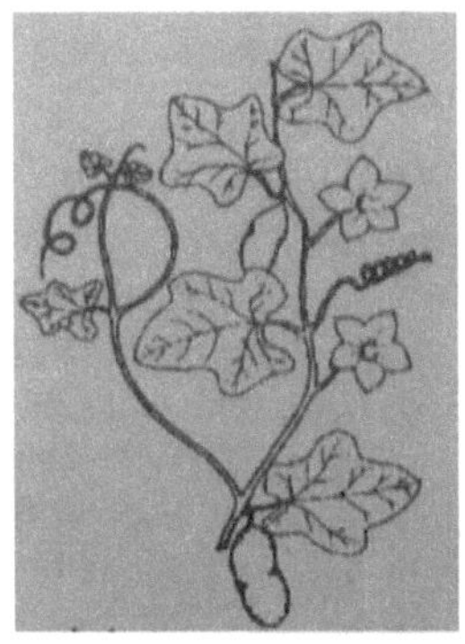

On *May 10, 1901, Jagadish Chandra Bose proved that plants are like any other life form.*

Sir J.C. Bose proved that plants have a definite life cycle, and a reproductive system and are aware of their surroundings. The demonstration took place at the Royal Society in London, England.

Bose showed how plants behave differently under different environmental factors such as temperature, chemicals, electricity, gases, and humidity. He showed the electrical nature of conduction among several stimuli in plants, which were earlier believed to have a chemical nature.

Bose was the first to study the action of microwaves in plant tissues and the changes in the plant cell membrane potential. Through this study, **he proved that plants are sensitive to pain and affection.**

The idea of plants communicating to humans through **a "subtle voice"** refers to the concept that plants possess unique qualities and characteristics that can be observed and understood with sensitivity and attentiveness. While plants do not communicate in the same way that humans or animals do (e.g., through vocalizations), they exhibit subtle signals and behaviors that convey important information about their health, needs, and interactions with the environment. Here are some aspects related to the idea of plants communicating through a subtle voice:

1. **Visual Cues:** Plants often provide visual cues that convey their condition and requirements. For example, wilting leaves may indicate a need for water, while yellowing leaves could signal nutrient deficiencies. By observing these visual signs, gardeners and botanists can interpret what plants are "saying" about their well-being.

2. **Scent and Fragrance:** Many plants emit scents and fragrances that can have practical or emotional effects on humans. For instance, aromatic herbs like lavender and rosemary not only enhance the sensory experience but also have calming or invigorating properties. The presence of certain scents can also indicate pollination or the presence of specific chemicals in the environment.

3. **Sound and Vibration:** While plants do not produce sounds audible to the human ear, some studies suggest that plants may respond to vibrations and acoustic

signals. For example, the rustling of leaves in the wind or the buzzing of insects near flowers may create subtle vibrations that influence plant growth and development.

4. **Chemical Signalling:** Plants release a variety of chemicals into the air and soil that serve as signals to other organisms, including humans. These chemicals can attract pollinators, repel herbivores, or communicate with neighboring plants.

5. **Energy Sensitivity:** Some individuals believe in the concept of "energy sensitivity," which suggests that humans can perceive subtle energies emitted by plants. **Practices like meditation, energy healing**, or mindfulness in nature are said to enhance this sensitivity, allowing individuals to connect more deeply with plants and their environment.

6. **Cultural and Spiritual Significance:** Plants hold cultural and spiritual significance in many societies. Indigenous cultures often have rich traditions of plant knowledge and use plants in rituals, ceremonies, and healing practices. The symbolism associated with specific plants reflects deep cultural insights and connections.

7. **Intuitive Understanding:** Many gardeners and plant enthusiasts develop an intuitive understanding of plants over time. They may sense when a plant needs attention or observe subtle changes in growth patterns that reveal underlying conditions. This intuitive

connection is cultivated through experience and attentiveness.

8. **Biophilia:** The concept of biophilia, popularized by biologist E.O. Wilson, suggests that humans have an innate affinity for nature and living organisms, including plants. This natural inclination fosters empathy and appreciation for plants, enabling a deeper understanding of their **"subtle voice."**

9. **With a Primitive eye-like structure, Plants can see, a unique adaptation:** Of late, in the uncharted region of Karachi, nestled in the tranquillity of Lake Samsara, a team of botanists made a discovery that challenged the foundations of plant evolution. They discovered a plant that had developed a primitive eye-like structure, a unique adaptation, unlike anything seen before in the plant kingdom. This plant, named *Ocalaflora samsara*, is a type of sundew, a carnivorous plant species known for its sticky, gland-tipped tentacles, which they use to trap insects. It boasts a unique organ that mimics the functionality of an eye, complete with a biological lens and a structure reminiscent of a pupil. ***The lens of this eye is made from a transparent layer of specialized cells that have a high-water content, while the pupil is a concentrated area of photo-sensitive cells (vide- photo below).***

The botanists theorize that this evolution was driven by the plant's need to survive in the dense, competitive environment of Lake Samsara. This remarkable discovery provides a compelling insight into how plants can adapt and evolve in response to their environment. It opens up a new field of scientific exploration and revolutionizing our understanding of plant perception and adaptation.

Photographs showing the Eye like the structure of a plant named ***Oculoflora samsara***

The botanists theorize that this evolution was driven by the plant's need to survive in the dense, competitive environment of Lake Samsara. This remarkable discovery provides a compelling insight into how plants can adapt and evolve in response to their environment. It opens up a new field of scientific exploration and revolutionizing our understanding of plant perception and adaptation.

In summary, the idea of plants communicating through a subtle voice underscores the depth and complexity of plant life. By cultivating awareness, sensitivity, and intuition, humans can develop meaningful connections with plants and gain valuable insights into their world.

Chapter 3: Key Takeaways

1. It was J C Bose's 1901 demonstration at the Royal Society in London that changed that perception and proved that plants are like any other life form. Bose demonstrated that plants possess life cycles, reproductive systems, and awareness of their surroundings. His invention, the Crescograph, revealed plant movements and sensitivities to various stimuli, challenging prior beliefs.

2. A recent discovery of a plant with an eye-like structure in Lake Samsara highlights the adaptability of plants to their environments. Overall, understanding the subtle communication of plants requires sensitivity and intuition, offering valuable insights into their world and potential for scientific exploration.

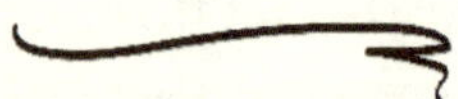

Chapter 4: The Secret life of plants

I quote a few lines from the book "The Secret Life of Plants by "Tompkins, Peter; Bird, Christopher:

"There is nothing lovelier on this planet than a flower, nor more essential than a plant. The true matrix of human life is the greensward covering Mother Earth. Without green plants, we would neither breathe nor eat. On the undersurface of every leaf, a million movable lips are engaged in devouring carbon dioxide and expelling oxygen."

"All the food, drink, intoxicants, drugs, and medicines that keep a man alive and, if properly used, radiantly healthy are ours through the sweetness of photosynthesis. Sugar produces all our starches, fats, oils, waxes, and cellulose. From crib to a coffin, man relies on cellulose as the basis for his shelter, clothing, fuel, fibers, basketry, cordage, musical instruments, and the paper on which he scribbles his philosophy."

The concept of plants having a "secret life" often refers to the intriguing and lesser-known aspects of their biology and behavior beyond what meets the eye. While plants may seem static compared to animals, they possess remarkable abilities and exhibit complex behaviors that contribute to their survival and adaptation. Here are some fascinating findings that contribute to the idea of plants having a **"secret life"**:

1. Root Communication and Networking:

Underground, plants engage in a sophisticated form of communication and networking through their root systems. Mycorrhizal fungi create extensive networks that connect multiple plants, enabling the exchange of nutrients, water, and chemical signals between individuals. This interconnected web of roots and fungi forms a "wood wide web" that facilitates cooperation and mutual support among plants.

The finding of the knitting of the root system of the redwood - Sequoia on the east coast of California is still surprising. *I quote from a speech delivered by one of the Monks in America.*

"A few years ago, I was walking with a friend in the Muir Woods, which is just close to San Francisco It's a redwood forest. We came upon a park ranger; He was explaining to some tourists the secret of the forest. He said that the Sequoia or Redwood trees (Sequoia sempervirans) are the largest trees on the planet. Some of them are hundreds or even thousands of years old. But interestingly, their roots do not grow deep and then he said that these trees have been saved for centuries and centuries, enduring massive wind storms,

frigid blizzards, and devastating earthquakes. And without deep roots, how do they keep standing? Then the Ranger paused so that we could ponder this will start to reveal to us the underground secret movement for history.

And being from the 60s, I like underground things. So, I was very attempting. He said that the roots under the ground reach outward seeking the roots of other Redwood trees. ***And when they meet, they intertwine, making a permanent bond with each other. In this way, all the Redwood trees in the entire forest are either directly or indirectly giving support to each other Unity is their strength. They reach out to care for each other.*** *Even the little newborn baby red ones, their little, tiny boots are given shelter by the ancient Giants in the Mill Woods, nature has given humanity a very crucial lesson.* ***There is real strength in our willingness to care for and support each other.*** *They'll be takers of dividing property Wisdom is to understand the simple,* ***universal principle that you're giving receive by getting things by giving.*** *We make a life The spiritual evolution of a society can be understood when people love people and use things. But, all too often, in today's world, it's just the opposite People use people and they love things"*

We need to live together, knitting with each other, and extending health to each other as redwoods do this. **But today, in contrast, we never leave wars with lethal weapons causing the suffering and death of our fellow human beings. While Plants never do this kind of**

genocide. They even help and allow the smaller plants to grow under their shades with good health.

2. Chemical Signaling and Defense:

Plants produce a wide array of chemicals, including volatile organic compounds (VOCs), which serve as signals to communicate with other plants and organisms. When attacked by herbivores, plants release specific VOCs that can alert neighboring plants to the presence of threats, prompting them to activate defense mechanisms such as producing toxins or repellent compounds.

Plant defense against herbivory or host-plant resistance (HPR) is a range of adaptations evolved by plants that improve their survival and reproduction by reducing the impact of herbivores. Many plants produce secondary metabolites, known as allelochemicals, that influence the behavior, growth, or survival of herbivores.

3. Memory and Learning:

Recent studies suggest that plants can "remember" past experiences and adjust their responses accordingly. For example, plants exposed to repetitive mechanical stimulation (e.g., wind or touch) may develop thicker stems or more robust structures to withstand future disturbances.

In plant biology, plant memory describes the ability of a plant to retain information from experienced stimuli and respond at a later time. For example, some plants have been observed to raise their leaves synchronously with the rising of the sun e.g. ***Samania saman*** tree. Other plants produce new leaves in the spring after overwintering.

4. Electrical Signaling:

Plants use electrical signals to transmit information within their tissues. This electrical communication plays a role in coordinating growth, development, and responses to environmental stimuli. The electrical signals do not only trigger rapid leaf movements in 'sensitive' plants such as *Mimosa pudica* or *Dionaea muscipula* but also do physiological processes in ordinary plants.

5. Symbiotic Relationships:

Plants form intricate symbiotic relationships with various organisms, including mycorrhizal fungi, nitrogen-fixing bacteria, and pollinators. These relationships enhance nutrient uptake, protect against pathogens, and facilitate reproduction, highlighting the interconnectedness of plant life with other organisms. (e.g. Alder (*Alnus glutinosa, Casuarina equisetifolia,*), etc have a symbiotic relationship with nitrogen-fixing bacteria. The list of nitrogen-fixing plants for agriculture is also quite versatile.

6. Behavioural Responses:

Plants exhibit behavioral responses to their environment. For instance, certain plants can adjust their leaf orientation or growth patterns in response to changes in light intensity or direction. (e.g. **Sunflower- *Helianthus annus***). ***Cissus quadrangularis*** extend their tendrils to get support from nearby plants of any other material.

Similarly, Sundews-Drosera, which is commonly known as the sundews, is one of the largest genera of carnivorous plants, with at least 194 species. These members of the family Droseraceae lure, capture, and digest insects using stalked mucilaginous glands. Further, Nepenthes is a genus of carnivorous plants, also known as tropical pitcher plants, or ***Nepenthes khasiana*** in the monotypic family Nepenthaceae.

7. Longevity and Resilience:

Many plants exhibit remarkable longevity and resilience. Some trees can live for thousands of years, enduring harsh environmental conditions and natural disasters. This longevity reflects the ability of plants to adapt, repair, and regenerate over time.

Our Average life expectancy varies from 60 to 80 years. For a few, it may cross even a hundred or a few more years but not comparable with the average life expectancy of trees. A shortlist of such trees is available from all over the world whose life expectancy was estimated to vary more than 5000 to 10000 years.

Here is an example of a few such trees.

1The General Sherman Tree (*Sequoia sempervirens*) Redwoods. About 2,000 years old and is a giant among giants. Located in Sequoia National Park, USA	**2. The Largest & Oldest Teak tree (*Tectona grandis*) in the World:** Estimated Age: Maybe 4000 years? at Parambikulam Tiger Reserve, Kerala, seen in June 2012. This Great Teak Tree is 39.98M in height & is 7.02M at GBH as measured during 1994-95. The Tree is declared as " Mahavriksha" by Govt of India.
3. Bristlecone Pine (*Pinus longaeva*): Name: Methuselah Location: White Mountains, California, USA Estimated Age: Over 4,800 years	**4. Giant Sequoia (*Sequoiadendron giganteum*):** Name: Prometheus (formerly) Location: Wheeler Peak, Nevada, USA (destroyed in 1964) Estimated Age: Over 4,900 years (before its destruction)
5.Yew (*Taxus baccata*): Name: Llangernyw Yew Location: Conwy, Wales Estimated Age: Over 4,000 to 5,000 years	**6. Olive Tree (Olea europaea): Name: Olive Tree of Vouves** Location: Crete, Greece Estimated Age: Over 2,000 to 3,000 years
7.Baobab (Adansonia): Name: Panke Baobab Location: Maun, Botswana (collapsed in 2017) Estimated Age: Over 6,000 years (before its collapse) **9.Quaking Aspen (Populus tremuloides): Name: Pando** Location: Fishlake National Forest, Utah, USA Estimated Age: Over 80,000 years (though Pando is a clonal colony, and individual stems may not be as old)	**8. Sugi (Cryptomeria japonica): Name: Jomon Sugi** Location: Yakushima, Japan Estimated Age: Over 2,170 to 7,200 years

8. Communication with Pollinators:

Plants have evolved specialized adaptations to attract and communicate with pollinators. They produce colorful flowers, enticing scents, and nutritious rewards (e.g., nectar) to ensure successful pollination and reproductive success.

The concept of plants having a dynamic "secret life" underscores their remarkable abilities to perceive, communicate, and interact with their surroundings, contributing to the complexity and beauty of the natural world. Understanding and appreciating these hidden aspects of plant biology deepen our respect for the vital role that plants play in sustaining ecosystems and supporting life on Earth.

Chapter -4: Key Takeaways

1. The passage explores the concept of plants having a "secret life," delving into lesser-known aspects of their biology and behavior. It highlights fascinating findings such as root communication and networking through mycorrhizal fungi, chemical signaling for defense, memory and learning capabilities, electrical signaling for coordination, symbiotic relationships with other organisms, behavioral responses to the environment, longevity and resilience, and communication with pollinators.

2. These revelations challenge traditional perceptions of plants as passive organisms, revealing their dynamic and multifaceted nature. The "secret life" of plants includes their ability to perceive, communicate, and interact with their surroundings in sophisticated ways. Understanding and appreciating these hidden aspects of plant biology deepen our respect for their vital role in sustaining ecosystems and supporting life on Earth.

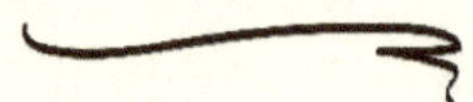

PART- III: GLOBAL DISTRIBUTION OF FORESTS, THEIR TYPES, COMPOSITION AND THREATS

Chapter 5: Worldwide Distribution of Forests-their Types, Compositions, and location

The European countries have a maximum of 25.07 % mainly with Temperate types of forests with coniferous trees as they are located in mid-latitudes to towards the polar region.

South America possesses 20.8% forest cover mainly with Tropical Rain Forests full of biodiversity and high-density valuable forests covering mainly Brazil, Bolivia, and Peru as they are near the equatorial regions.

Africa is almost without much forest cover except for the Democratic Republic of Congo, Angola, Zambia, and Tanzania have Tropical rainforests because of their nearness to the equatorial zone and cover 15.68% of forests.

Asian countries have tropical, sub-tropical, and Mangrove Forest cover of 15.34% with China, and India being the main countries. The rest covers Oceania with only 4.56 % of forest.

Status and trends in forest areas:

Forest ecosystems are a critical component of the world's biodiversity as many forests are more biodiverse than other ecosystems.

The area covered by forests is thus one of the indicators of the Sustainable Development Goal of "Life on land".

According to FRA 2020, forests currently cover 30.8 percent of the global land area (FAO, 2020). The total forest area is 4.06 billion hectares or approximately 0.5 ha per person, but forests are not equally distributed around the globe.

More than half of the world's forests are found in only five countries (the Russian Federation, Brazil, Canada, the United States of America, and China) and two-thirds (66 percent) of forests are found in ten countries **(vide Figure 5.1).**

Figure 5.1 -Global Distribution of Forests showing the Ten Countries with the Largest Forest Area, 2020 (Million Hectares and % of World's Forests)

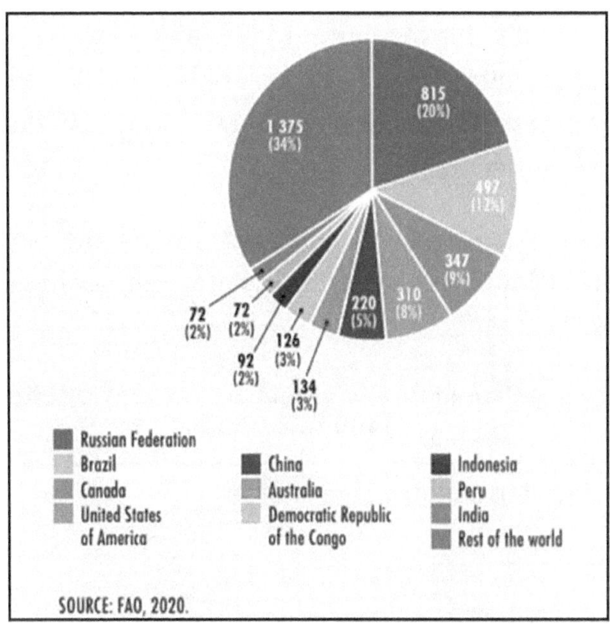

Map 5.2- Shows the Share of the global forest area, in 2020 on the map below:

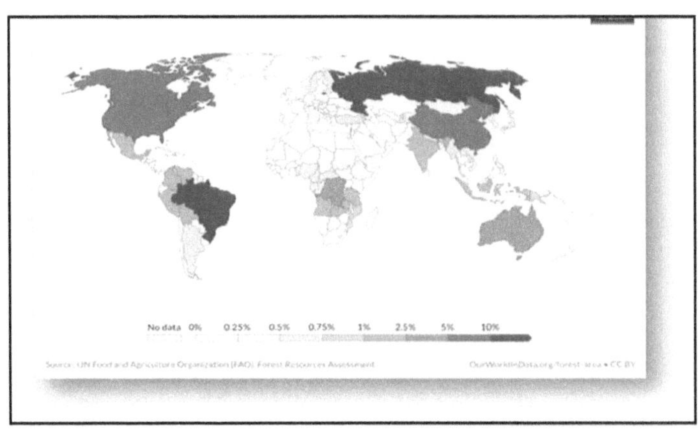

Global Forest Types, Plant Compositions, and their location:

The world's forests are diverse and can be broadly categorized into several major types based on their characteristics, geographical locations, and the predominant plant species they contain.

The main types of forests found around the world are narrated below based on their floral compositions, and biodiversity.

Figure 5.3-Proportion of global forest area by climatic domain, 2020

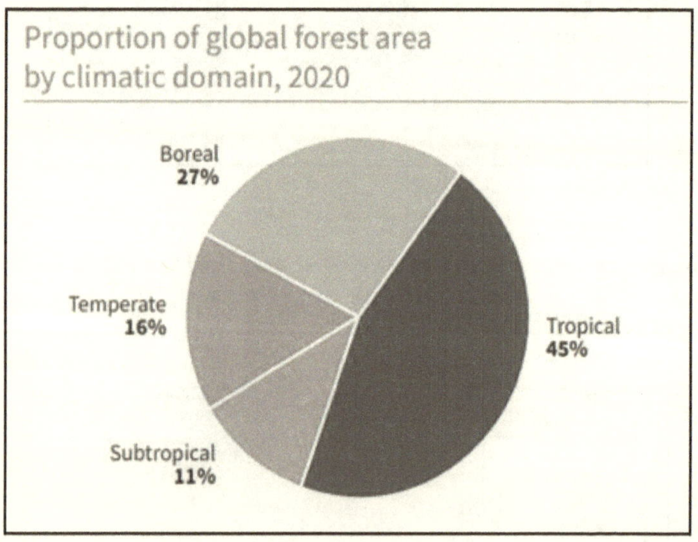

1. **Tropical Rainforests:** Located around the equator in regions such as the Amazon Basin, Congo Basin, and Southeast Asia. High temperatures, high humidity, and consistent rainfall resulted in extremely diverse flora and fauna. Characterized by a dense and diverse array

of plant life, including towering trees like mahogany, teak, and ebony. Epiphytes, such as orchids and bromeliads, are common, and the understory is filled with ferns and various shrubs. Home to many endemic and endangered species. Logging, Agriculture, Infrastructure Development, and Mining are the Major Causes of deforestation.

2. **Temperate Forests:** Found in temperate regions, including parts of North America, Europe, and East Asia. Moderate temperatures with distinct seasons. Eastern Deciduous Forest in North America, European Temperate Forests, and East Asian Forests. Dominated by deciduous trees that shed their leaves in the fall, including oak, maple, beech, and hickory. The understory often includes flowering plants, ferns, and mosses. Rich in bird species, mammals like deer and bears, etc.

3. **Boreal Forests (Taiga):** Located in High latitudes, mostly in the Northern Hemisphere. Northern regions of North America, Europe, and Asia. Cold temperatures, coniferous trees (evergreen needle-leaved), and a relatively short growing season. Siberian Taiga, Canadian Boreal Forest, Scandinavian Taiga. Predominantly composed of coniferous trees like spruce, fir, and pine. Ground vegetation includes mosses, lichens, and hardy shrubs. It is inhabited by species such as moose, wolves, and migratory birds.

4. **Temperate Rainforests:** Found along the western coasts of North America, including the Pacific Northwest, and parts of New Zealand and Chile. Mild temperatures, high rainfall, and evergreen trees. More temperate than tropical rainforests. *Characterized* by dense vegetation of evergreen trees such as redwoods and Douglas firs. Mosses, ferns, and other understorey vegetation thrive in the moist environment. Diverse wild fauna such as bears, cougars, and various bird species are found here.

5. **Mediterranean Forests:** Located around the Mediterranean Sea and other regions with a Mediterranean climate. Mediterranean Basin, California Chaparral, South African Fynbos. Hot, dry summers and mild, wet winters. They are dominated by evergreen trees and shrubs.

6. **Montane Forests:** Located in Mountainous regions at various latitudes. Montane Rainforests in the Andes, Rocky Mountains, and Himalayan Montane Forests. Floral Composition varies with altitude but may include a mix of coniferous and broadleaf trees. Alpine plants adapted to harsh conditions, such as lichens and dwarf shrubs, become prevalent at higher elevations. Species in these forests have adapted to the challenging conditions of high altitudes.

7. **Dry Forests:** Situated in Arid and semi-arid regions. Found in regions with a pronounced dry season, such as parts of Africa, Asia, and the Americas. Thorn Forests

in Africa, Dry Forests in Australia. Typically consists of drought-resistant trees and shrubs, such as acacias, baobabs, and succulent plants. Animals like camels, kangaroos, and various reptiles are from here.

8. **Polar Ice Cap and Tundra:** Located around the polar regions, with cold temperatures, permafrost, and low-lying vegetation. Arctic Tundra, Antarctic Tundra. These forest types are critical for global biodiversity, climate regulation, and the well-being of ecosystems. They face various threats, including deforestation, climate change, and habitat destruction, emphasizing the importance of conservation efforts.

Chapter- 5: Key Takeaways

1. European forests: Cover about 25.07% of the region, primarily temperate with coniferous trees, due to their mid-latitude to polar location.

2. South American and African forests: Encompassing 20.8% of the region, mainly tropical rainforests rich in biodiversity, concentrated in Brazil, Bolivia, and Peru. *African forests*: Except for regions like the Democratic Republic of Congo, Angola, Zambia, and Tanzania, which hold tropical rainforests, Africa has minimal forest cover.

3. Asian and Oceania forests: Tropical, sub-tropical, and mangrove areas, covering 15.34%, with China and India as key contributors. Oceania forests: Account for only 4.56% of global forests.

Overall, forests play a crucial role in biodiversity conservation and climate regulation but face threats like deforestation and climate change, highlighting the importance of conservation efforts.

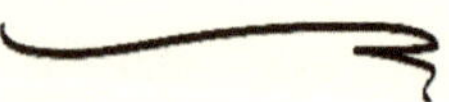

Chapter 6: Global Threat Status of Plants and Forests

i) Threat Status of Plants

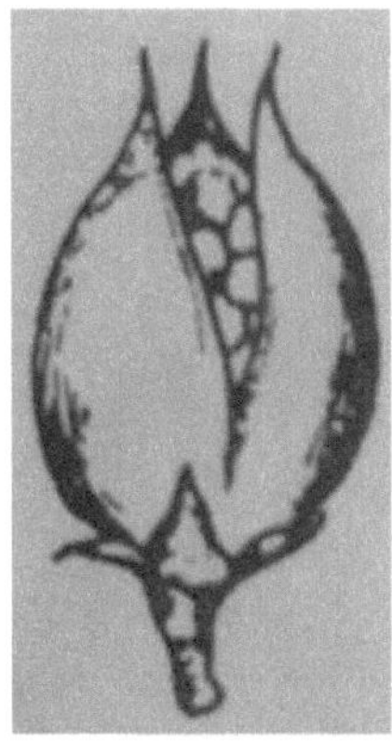

The species extinction rate has increased many-fold over the years due to the ever-increasing human population and anthropogenic activities, bringing to the forefront the '**Sixth mass extinction' crisis** (Shivanna 2020).

The estimated number of threatened species in Kingdom Plantae, Animalia, Chromista, and Fungi, globally and in India as per the IUCN assessment (IUCN 2020) is shown in **Figure -6.1).**

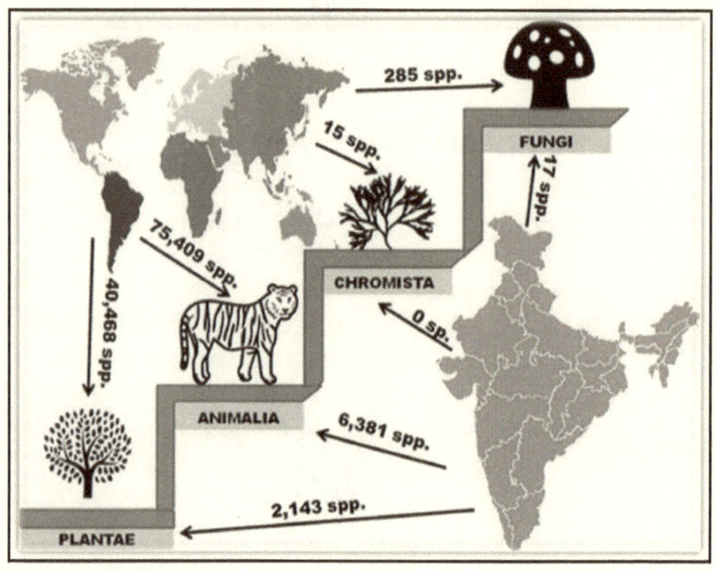

The numerical values mentioned on the arrows indicate the number of threatened species (Source: IUCN 2020). More than 50% of the world's plant species are endemic to 35 Global Biodiversity Hotspots (GBH). These hotspots shelter a large number of endemic species, which are facing an increasing threat of extinction (Hazarika et al. 2016).

On a global basis, IUCN has estimated that about 13.49% of the world's vascular plants (3,00,000 species), totaling about 40,468 species are under varying degrees of threat. Break-up details are shown in Table 6.1 It is estimated that India has 10.45% of global floral diversity. In India, about 11.53% of vascular plants (18,532), totaling about 2,142 species are red-listed. Details are given in Table 6.2 below.

Table 6.1 Number of Families, Genera, and Globally Threatened Vascular Plants

	World Total	Extinct		Threatened plant species			Lower Risk plant species			
		EX	EW	CR	EN	VU	LR /cd	NT	LC	DD
Total Species Count	3,00,000									
No, of Threatened Plant species	40,468	123	37	3325	6063	7072	171	2500	18403	2774

Table 6.2 Status of Threatened Vascular Plants in India

	India Total	Extinct		Threatened plant species			Lower Risk plant species			
		EX	EW	CR	EN	VU	LR/cd	NT	LC	DD
Total Species Count	18,532									
No, of Threatened Plant species	2143	6	2	86	191	155	1	54	1545	103

Table 6 1. and 6.2: Number of plant species threatened as per IUCN estimation (EX: Extinct; EW- Extinct in the Wild; CR-Critically Endangered; EN: Endangered; VU: Vulnerable; LR/cd: Lower Risk-Conservation Dependent; NT: Near threatened; LC: Least concern; DD; Data deficient (Source: IUCN 2020)

More than 60,000 different tree species are known, more than 20,000 of which have been included in the IUCN Red List of Threatened Species, and more than 8,000 of these are assessed as globally threatened. More than 1 400 tree species are assessed as critically endangered and in urgent need of conservation action. Some 8 percent of assessed forest plants, 5 percent of forest animals, and 5 percent of fungi found in forests are currently listed as critically endangered.

The forest-specialist index, based on 455 monitored populations of 268 forest mammals, amphibians, reptiles, and birds, fell by 53 percent between 1970 and 2014, an annual rate of decline of 1.7 percent. This highlights the increased risk of these species becoming vulnerable to extinction.

Human health and well-being are closely associated with forests. More than 28,000 plant species are currently recorded as being of medicinal use.

Visits to forest environments can have positive impacts on human physical and mental health and it is being regularly practiced by Japanese people as a **forest bath.**

Yet, forests also pose health risks. Forest-associated diseases include malaria, American trypanosomiasis, African trypanosomiasis (sleeping sickness), HIV, and Ebola.

The majority of new infectious diseases affecting humans, including the SARS-CoV2 virus that caused the current COVID-19 pandemic, are zoonotic and increase human exposure to wildlife.

On a global basis, IUCN has estimated that about 13.49% of the world's vascular plants (3,00,000 species), totaling about 40,468 species are under varying degrees of threat.

ii) Global threat Status of Forests

In 2009, two-thirds of the world's forests were located in just 10 countries: Russia, Brazil, Canada, the United States, China, Australia, the Democratic Republic of the Congo, Indonesia, India, and Peru.

Rates and causes of deforestation vary from region to region around the world. In decades since 1990, South America and Africa have shown the greatest loss of global forest area.

Global annual deforestation is estimated to total 13.7 million hectares a year. Half of the area experiencing deforestation consists of new forests. In addition to direct human-induced deforestation, growing forests have also been affected by climate change.

In 2010, the world had 3.92 billion hectares (ha) of tree cover, extending over 30% of its land area. In 2022, it lost 22.8 million ha of tree cover (FAO). In 2020, the world had a total forest area of 4.06 billion ha, which was 31 percent of the total land area.

The tropical domain has the largest proportion of the world's forests (45 percent), followed by the boreal, temperate, and subtropical domains. More than half (54 percent) of the world's forests are in only five countries – the Russian Federation (20.1%), Brazil (12.2%), Canada (8.6%), the USA (7.6%), and China (5.4%).

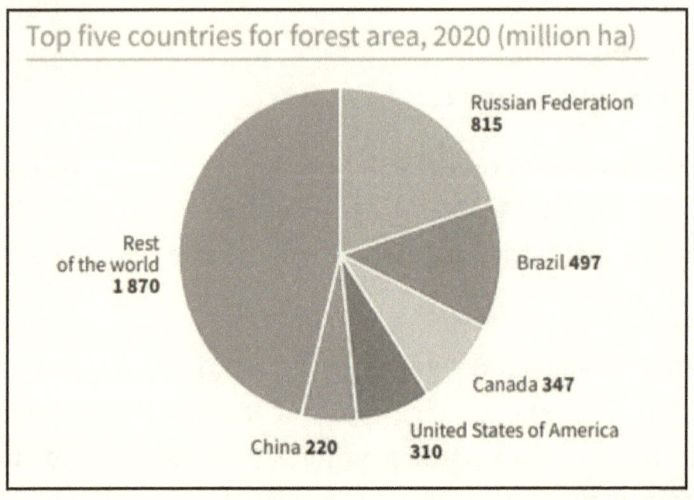

Many of the world's forests are being damaged and degraded or are disappearing altogether.

Their capacity to provide tangible goods, such as fiber, food, and medicines, as well as essential ecological services, is under greater threat than ever before.

According to the World Resource Institute in Washington, between 2000 and 2020 the world lost 101 million hectares (Mah) of tree cover, mostly tropical and subtropical forests (92%) **Vide in Figure 6.3.**

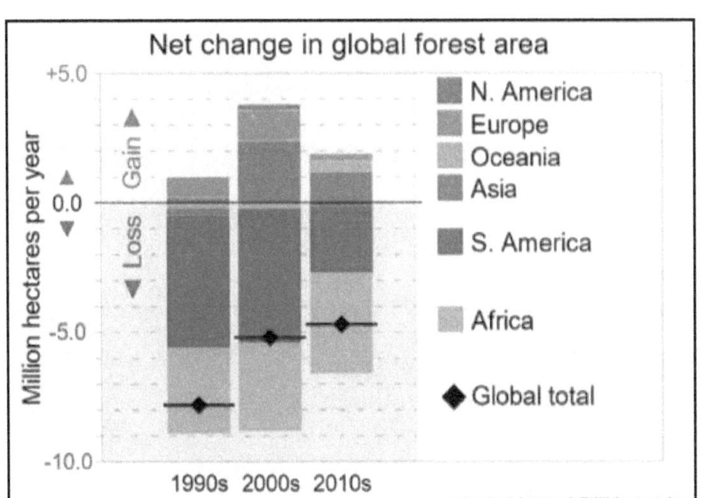

Chapter 6: Key Takeaways

1. **Threat Status of Plants:** The extinction rate of species, including plants, has soared due to human activities, leading to a global crisis known as the 'sixth mass extinction.' Over 50% of plant species are endemic to 35 Global Biodiversity Hotspots, making them particularly vulnerable. According to the IUCN, approximately 13.49% of the world's vascular plants, totaling about 40,468 species, are under threat, with India hosting 10.45% of global floral diversity, of which 11.53% are red-listed.

2. **Global Threat of Forests** mainly concentrated in ten countries, are shrinking globally, with South America and Africa experiencing significant losses. Annual deforestation amounts to 13.7 million hectares, with

climate change exacerbating the situation. In 2022, the world had 4.06 billion hectares of forest cover, accounting for 31% of the land area. However, deforestation continues to jeopardize their ecological services and biodiversity. Between 2000 and 2020, the world lost 101 million hectares of tree cover, mostly in tropical and subtropical regions.

Overall, it emphasizes the urgent need for conservation efforts globally to mitigate these threats and preserve biodiversity and ecosystem integrity.

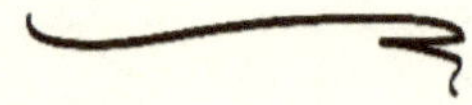

PART -IV: CAUSES OF DEFORESTATION, IT'S EFFECTS AND STRATEGIC PLAN TO CONTROL

Chapter 7: Deforestation and its Direct Causes

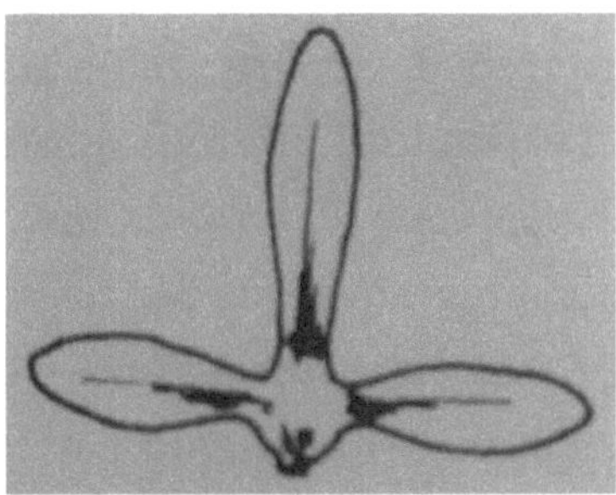

Forests cover almost a third of the earth's land surface and provide many environmental benefits. Forest resources can provide long-term national economic benefits.

Deforestation is the conversion of forest to an alternative permanent non-forested land use such as agriculture, grazing, or urban development.   Deforestation is primarily a concern for the developing countries of the tropics as it is shrinking areas of the tropical forests causing loss of biodiversity and enhancing the greenhouse effect.

Forest degradation occurs when the ecosystem functions of the forest are degraded but where the area remains forested rather than cleared.

Thirty percent of the earth's land area or about 3.9 billion hectares is covered by forests. It was estimated that the original forest cover was approximately six billion hectares.

The Russian Federation, Brazil, Canada, the United States of America, and China were the most forest-rich countries accounting for 53 percent of the total forest area of the globe.

The forest area remained fairly stable in North and Central America while it expanded in Europe during the past decade. Asian continents especially India and China due to their large-scale afforestation program in the last decade registered a net gain in the forest area. Conversely, South America, Africa, and Oceania registered the net annual loss of forest area (Anon., 2010; 2011a).

A. World deforestation

Deforestation is no longer significant in developed temperate countries. In most instances, developed nations are located in temperate domains and developing nations in tropical domains. Tropical rainforests capture the most attention but 60 percent of the deforestation that occurred in tropical forests during 1990-2010. The FAO FRA 2001 and 2010 reports indicate considerable deforestation in the world during 1990-2010 but this was almost entirely confined to tropical regions.

We see massive differences in how important each driver of deforestation is across the world.

i). 95% of the world's deforestation occurs in the tropics. In Latin America and Southeast Asia in particular, commodity-driven deforestation – mainly the clearance of forests to grow crops such as palm oil and soybean, and pasture for beef production – accounts for almost two-thirds of forest loss.

Figure 7.1-Nearly all global deforestation occurs in the tropics

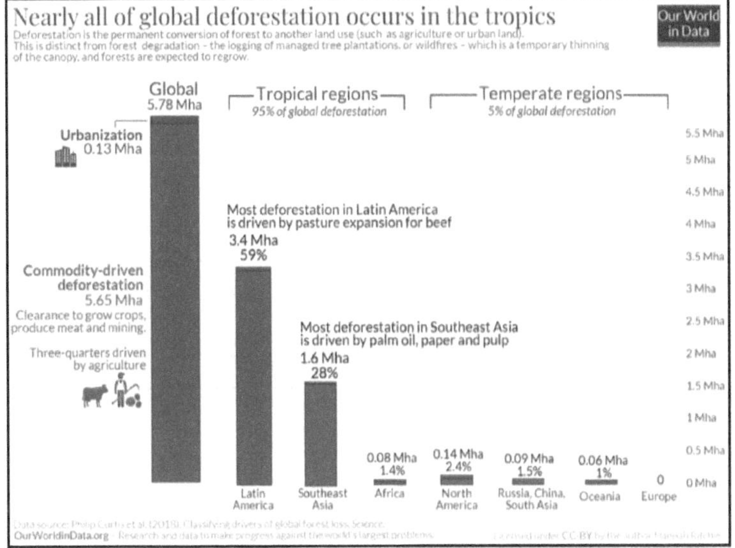

ii). A summary of deforestation during the decades 1990-2010-2020 was considerable deforestation in the world, and this was almost confined to tropical regions.

a). The natural and human-induced changes have different impacts on forest biodiversity. Africa had the highest net loss of forest area in 2010–2020, with a loss of 3.94 million hectares per year, followed by South America with 2.60 million hectares per year (**Fig.7.2)**

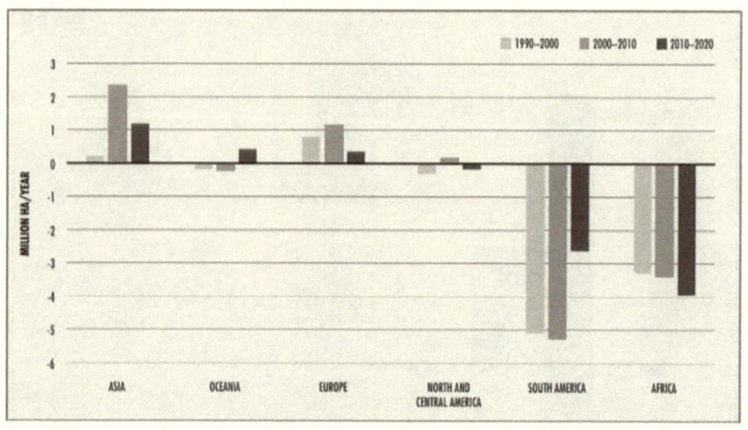

b). Since 1990, Africa has reported an increase in the rate of net loss, while South America's losses have decreased substantially, more than halving since 2010 relative to the previous decade.

c). Asia showed the highest net gain in forest area in the period 2010–2020, followed by Oceania and Europe. Both Europe and Asia reported a net forest gain every ten years since 1990, although both regions show a substantial reduction in the rate of gain since 2010.

iii). South America with about four million hectares per year suffered the largest net loss of forests during the last decade followed by Africa with 3.4 million hectares annually and the least Oceania with seven lakh hectares annually.

iv). Both Brazil and Indonesia had the highest net loss of forest during the decade of 1990 but have significantly reduced their rate of loss after this decade.

v). The forest area in North and Central America remained stable and Europe continued to expand although at a slow rate during the past decade.

vi). Asia lost some six lakh hectares annually during the 1990s but gained more than 2.2 million hectares per year during the last decade.

vii). The ten countries with the largest net loss per year in the period 1990-2000 AD had a combined net loss of forest area of 7.9 million hectares per year. In the period 2000-2010 AD this was reduced to six million hectares per year as a result of reductions in Indonesia, Sudan, Brazil, and Australia.

viii). The area of other wooded land also decreased during the past two decades in Africa, Asia, and South America.

B. The causes of deforestation

To save forests, we need to know why they are being destroyed. Distinguishing between the agents of deforestation and its causes is very important to understanding the major determinants of deforestation.

i) The agents of deforestation are those slash and burn farmers, commercial farmers, ranchers, loggers, firewood collectors, infrastructure developers, and others who are cutting down the forests.

ii) Causes of deforestation are the **forces that motivate the agents to clear the forests.**

However, most of the existing literature typically distinguishes between two levels of specific factors **Direct and Indirect causes of deforestation.**

Direct agents and causes of deforestation, also typically referred to as sources of deforestation, first-level or proximate causes are relatively easy to identify but the indirect causes are usually the main drivers of deforestation.

This factor is substantially demonstrated by the conversion of forest land to other uses such as agriculture, infrastructure, urban development, industry, and others.

C. Direct Causes of Deforestation:

1. Expansion of farming land:

About 60 % of the clearing of tropical moist forests is for agricultural settlement with logging and other reasons like roads, urbanization, and Fuelwood accounting for the rest. Tropical forests are one of the last frontiers in the search for subsistence land for the most vulnerable people worldwide (Myers, 1992).

The expansion of agricultural land is generally viewed as the main source of deforestation contributing around 60 percent of total tropical deforestation.

Shifting agriculture is the clearing of forested land for raising or growing crops until the soil is exhausted of nutrients and then moving on to clear more forest.

Most reports indicate shifting agriculture as responsible for about one-half of tropical deforestation and some put it up to two-thirds. Shifting agriculture was greatest in Asia (about 30 %) but only about 15 percent over the whole tropical world.

Figure 7.3- Global forest loss: Deforestation vs. forest degradation

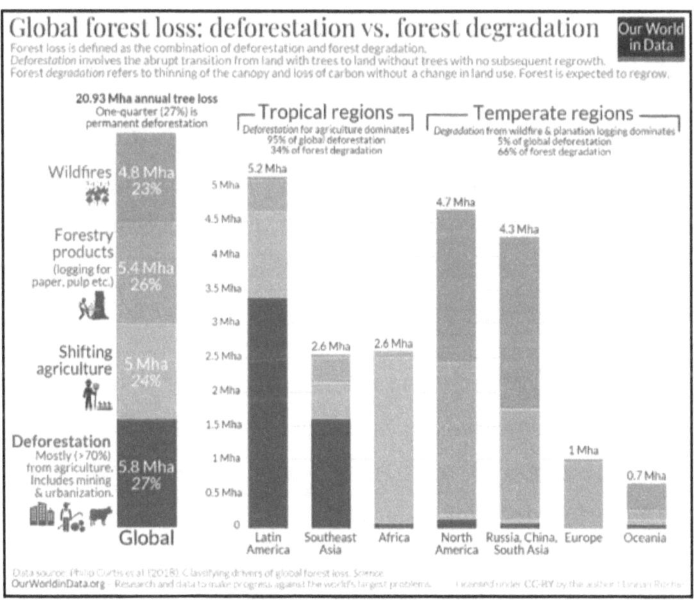

We see massive differences in how important each driver is across the world. 95% of the world's deforestation occurs in the tropics.

In contrast, most forest degradation – two-thirds of it – occurs in temperate countries.

2. Forest and other plantations:

Plantations are a positive benefit and should assist in reducing the rate of deforestation. The fact that plantations remove the timber pressure on natural forests does not translate eventually into less, but rather into more deforestation.

Tree crops and rubber in particular play a more important role in deforestation in Indonesia about one-half of the rubber plantations in the tropics are established on native forests cleared for the purpose.

3. Logging and Fuel Wood

Logging does not necessarily cause deforestation. However, logging can seriously degrade forests. Logging in Southeast Asia is more intensive and can be quite destructive. Logging provides access roads to follow-on settlers etc. Thus, Logging catalyzes deforestation.

Fuelwood gathering is often concentrated in tropical dry forests and degraded forest areas. In the drier areas of the tropics, Fuelwood gathering can be a major cause of deforestation and degradation.

4. Overgrazing

Overgrazing is more common in drier areas of the tropics where pastures degraded by overgrazing are subject to soil erosion. Clearcutting and overgrazing have turned large areas of Qinghai province in China into a desert.

Overgrazing is causing large areas of grasslands north of Beijing and in Inner Mongolia and Qinghai province to turn into a desert. The eastern edge of the Qinghai-Tibet plateau used to be so green and rich. But now the grass is disappearing and the sand is coming.

5. Fires

Fires are a major tool used in clearing the forest for shifting and permanent agriculture and for developing pastures. Based on the data available from 118 countries representing 65 percent of the global forest area, an average of 19.8 million hectares or one percent of all forests were reported to be significantly affected by fires.

6. Mining

Mining is a very intensive and very destructive way of deforestation. The area of land involved is quite small and it is not seen as a major cause of primary deforestation. Mining is a lucrative activity promoting development booms which may attract population growth with consequent deforestation.

The deforestation rate due to mining activities in Guyana from 2000 to 2008 increased 2.77 times. In the Philippines, mining, along with logging, has been among the forces behind the country's loss of forest cover.

Similarly, Nyamagari Hills in Orissa, India currently threatened by Vedanta Aluminium Corporation's plan to start bauxite mining will destroy 750 hectares of reserved forest.

Massive and unchecked mining of coal, iron ore, and bauxite in Jharkhand, India has caused large-scale deforestation and created a huge water scarcity (Anon., 2011b). A massive land acquisition that will deforest no less than 57,000 hectares of forest and displace 9,615 families. (Mullick and Griffiths. 2007).

7. Urbanization/industrialization & infrastructure:

Expanding cities and towns requires land to establish the infrastructures necessary to support the growing population which is done by clearing the forests.

Tropical forests are a major target of infrastructure developments for oil exploitation, logging concessions, hydropower dam construction etc.

The development of these infrastructure projects is of worldwide concern, since tropical forest clearing accounts for roughly 20 % of anthropogenic carbon emissions destroying globally significant carbon sinks, and around 21 % of tropical forests have been lost worldwide since 1980 (Bawa et al., 2004).

8. Air pollution:

Air pollution is associated with the degradation of some European and North American forests. The syndrome is called "Waldsterben" or forest death. In 1982, eight percent of all West German trees exhibited damage that rose to about 52 % by 1987 (Raloff, 1989) and half of the trees reported dying of Waldsterben in the Alps.

9. Wars and the role of the military:

It is well-established that military operations caused deforestation in many countries namely in the Vietnam War. El Salvador and elsewhere. Apart from military involvement in wars, the role of the military in deforestation has been documented in Southeast Asia and South America.

More recently, the war between Russia and Ukraine; Israel and Palestine caused huge damage to forests and plants and these wars are continuing to cause devastation of plants and forests.

10. Tourism:

National parks and sanctuaries beyond doubt protect the forests, but uncautioned and improper opening of these areas to the public for tourism is damaging. The national governments of tropical and sub-tropical countries adopt tourism as an easy way of making money sacrificing stringent management strategies.

In the Terai Duars of eastern India's foothill Himalayas, eco-tourism is encouraged without having adequate management plans.

Chapter 7: Key Takeaways

1. Forests cover about a third of the Earth's land and provide crucial environmental benefits. Deforestation, primarily occurring in tropical regions, results from

various direct causes including agricultural expansion, logging, plantations, overgrazing, fires, mining, urbanization/industrialization, air pollution, wars, and tourism. Developing countries in the tropics bear the brunt of deforestation, leading to loss of biodiversity and exacerbating climate change

2. Plantations, while intended to alleviate pressure on natural forests, can paradoxically contribute to deforestation. Deforestation poses significant environmental challenges, including loss of biodiversity, soil degradation, and climate change. Efforts to mitigate deforestation require addressing the underlying causes and promoting sustainable land use practices.

Chapter 8: Indirect Causes of Deforestation

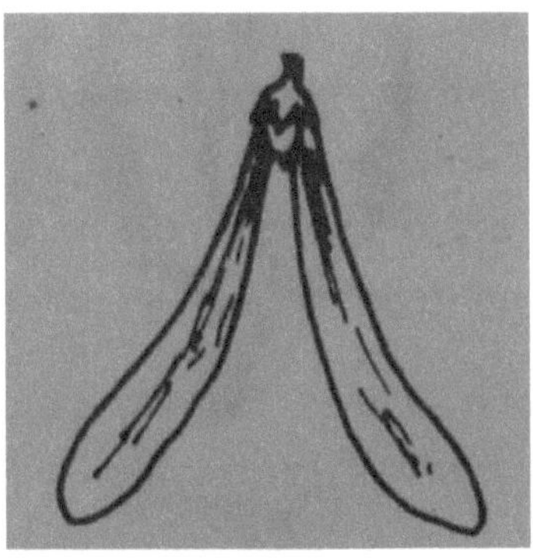

The World Rainforest Movement's 'Emergency Call to Action for the Forests and their Peoples' asserts that ***"deforestation is the inevitable result of the current social and economic policies being carried out in the name of development"*** (Anon., 1990d).

It is in the name of development that irrational and unscrupulous logging, cash crops, cattle ranching, large dams, colonization schemes, the dispossession of peasants and indigenous peoples, and the promotion of tourism are carried out.

Harrison Ngau, an Indigenous tribesman from Sarawak, Malaysia, and winner of the Goldman Environment Award in 1990 puts the cause of tropical deforestation like this,

"The roots of the problem of deforestation and waste of resources are located in the industrialized countries where most of our resources such as

tropical timber end up. The rich nations with one-quarter of the world's population consume four-fifths of the world's resources. It is the throw-away culture of the industrialized countries now advertised in and forced onto the Third World countries that are leading to the throwing away of the world. Such so-called progress leads to destruction and despair" (Anon., 1990d)!

Such a development leads to overconsumption which is the basic underlying cause of deforestation.

1. Colonialism:

Erstwhile colonies of colonial powers like Britain, France, Spain, and Portugal are now Third-world or developing nations that mostly have tropical rainforests were exploited for their natural resources, and their indigenous people's rights were destroyed by the colonial powers of rich industrialized nations.

Colonialism turned previously self-sufficient economies into zones of agricultural export production. This process continues even today in different forms of exploitation and the situation is worsening.

2. Exploitation by industrialized countries:

Wealthy countries or the erstwhile colonial powers having a deficit of their natural resources are mainly sustaining on the resources of the financially poorer countries which are generally natural resource-rich.

20% of the world's population uses 80 % of the world's resources.

Regrettably, the governments of these poor resource-rich countries also had generally adopted the same growth syndrome as their Western neighbors or their erstwhile colonial masters emphasizing maximizing exports, and revenues and exploiting their rich natural resources unsustainably for short-term gains. The problem is further worsened by the low price of most Third World exports being realized in the international market.

3. The debt burden:

Pursuing the guided development agenda, the financially poorer countries are on a heavy international debt and now feeling the urgency of repaying these huge debts due to escalating interest rates. Such a situation compels these debt-ridden poorer countries to exploit their rich natural resources including their forests partly to earn foreign exchange for servicing their debts.

For instance, the construction of roads for logging operations in some Southeast Asian countries was funded by Japanese aid which allowed the Japanese timber companies to exploit the forests of these countries.

4. Overpopulation and poverty:

Poverty and overpopulation are believed to be the main causes of forest loss according to international agencies such as FAO and intergovernmental bodies. It is generally believed by these organizations that they can solve the problem by encouraging development and trying to reduce population growth.

Conversely, the World Rainforest Movement and many other NGOs hold unrestrained development and the excessive consumption habits of rich industrialized countries directly responsible for most forest loss. However, there is good evidence that rapid population growth is a major indirect and over-arching cause of deforestation.

More people require more food and space which requires more land for agriculture and habitation. This in turn results in more clearing of forests.

Overpopulation is not a problem exclusive to Third World countries. An individual in an industrialized country is likely to consume in the order of sixty times as much of the world's resources as a person in a poor country.

The growing population in rich industrialized nations is therefore responsible for much of the exploitation of the earth and there is a clear link between the overconsumption in rich countries and deforestation in the tropics (Colchester and Lohmann, 1993).

Poverty and overpopulation are inextricably linked. Poverty, while undeniably responsible for much of the damage to rainforests, has to a large extent been brought about by the greed of the rich industrialized nations and the Third World elites who seek to emulate them.

The claim that overpopulation is the cause of deforestation is used by many governments and aid agencies as an excuse for inaction. In tropical countries, pressure from a human settlement comes about more from inequitable land distribution than from population pressure.

Generally, most of the land is owned by a small but powerful elite which displaces poor farmers into rainforest areas. So long as these elites maintain their grip on power, lasting land reform will be difficult to achieve and deforestation will continue unabated.

Therefore, **poverty is well considered to be an important underlying cause of forest conversion by small-scale farmers, and naturally forest-dense areas are frequently associated with high levels of poverty.**

5. Transmigration and colonisation schemes:

Transmigration of people to the forest frontier whether forced or voluntary due to development policy or dislocation from war is the major indirect cause of deforestation.

Moreover, governments and international aid agencies earlier believed that encouraging colonization and transmigration schemes into rainforest areas could alleviate the poverty of the areas in financially poorer countries.

In Indonesia, the Transmigration Program of 1974 caused annual deforestation of two lakh hectares.

6. Land rights, land tenure, and inequitable land distribution and resources:

Cultivators at the forest frontier often do not hold titles to land and are displaced by others who gain tenure over the land they occupy. This means they have to clear more forest to survive. Poorly defined tenure is generally bad for people and forests. In many countries, governments have nominal control of forests but are too weak to effectively regulate their use.

7. Economic causes - development/land conversion value, fiscal policies, markets, and consumerism:

One point of view is that development will increase land productivity and thereby reduce the need to clear forests to meet food requirements. Another is that development will produce further capital and incentive to expand and clear more forests.

Technological innovations make farming more profitable either prompting the expansion of farms into the forest or attracting new farmers to forest frontiers.

The global appropriation failures occur as in the case of tropical forests the benefits of biodiversity conservation and the value of the genetic pool in developing new medicines, crops, and pest control agents are poorly reflected in market allocations.

Rampant consumerism by the developed countries frequently has been claimed as a major reason for tropical deforestation. The opening of tropical countries to the world commodity markets accelerated deforestation. The products include coffee, sugar, bananas, cotton, and beef in Central America and oil palm, rubber, and timber in Southeast Asia.

(Vide Figure 8.1)

Figure 8.1-Deforestation Carbon emissions in international trade: who are the producers and who are the consumers?

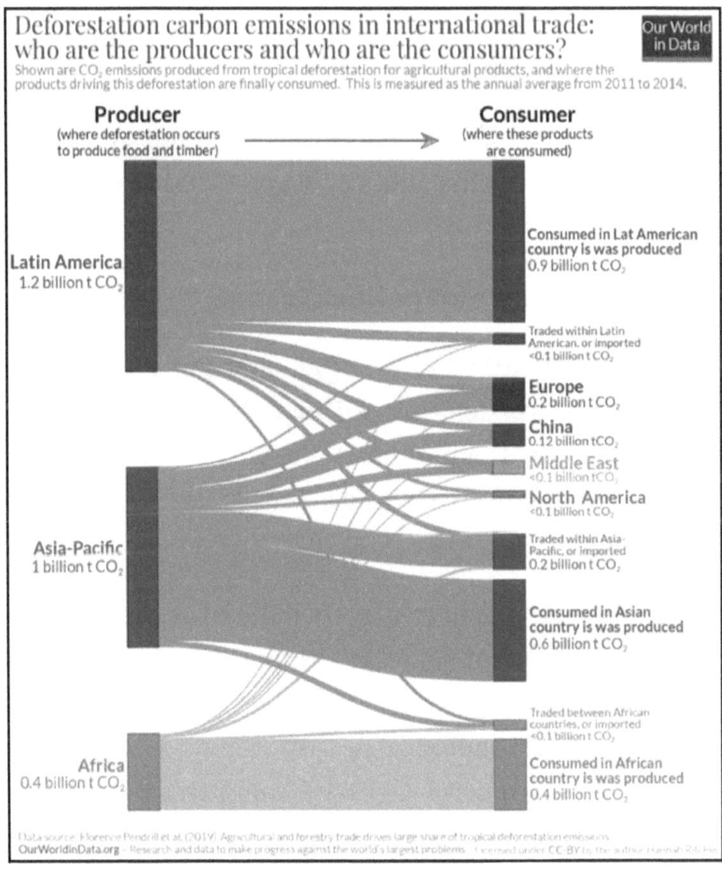

8. Undervaluing the forest:

Forests gain value only when cleared to obtain legal title through 'improvement'. The extraction of non-wood forest products has been suggested as a way to add value to the forest but it is not economical when compared to clearing options. If some means could be devised where those who benefit from the environmental values could pay the forest owners or agents of deforestation for them, then the option to not clear would become more competitive.

Alternatively, if the national governments value the environmental benefits, they could apply a tax or disincentives to clear.

9. Corruption and political cause:

The FAO identified forest crime and corruption as one of the main causes of deforestation in its 2001 report and warned that immediate attention has to be given to illegal activities and corruption in the world's forests in many countries (Anon., 2001b).

Illegal forest practices may include the approval of illegal contracts with private enterprises by forestry officers, illegal sale of harvesting permits, under-declaring volumes cut in public forests, underpricing of wood in concessions, harvesting of protected trees by commercial corporations, smuggling of forest products across borders and allowing illegal logging, processing forest raw materials without a license (Contreras-Hermosilla, 2000; 2001).

Chapter 8: Key Takeaways

1. Indirect causes of deforestation stem from social, economic, and political factors. Colonialism, exploitation by industrialized countries, and debt burden contribute to forest loss in developing nations. Overpopulation and poverty drive increased demand for land and resources, exacerbating deforestation.

2. Transmigration and colonization schemes displace indigenous peoples and increase pressure on forested areas. Inequitable land distribution and weak land tenure systems further fuel forest conversion. Economic factors such as development policies, market distortions, and consumerism prioritize short-term gains over environmental sustainability. Undervaluing forests and corruption also play significant roles in deforestation. Addressing these indirect causes requires addressing issues of equity, governance, and sustainable development on a global scale.

Chapter 9: Effects of Deforestation

Deforestation has multifaceted effects, including biodiversity loss, habitat destruction, and human-animal conflicts.

1. Decreased biodiversity, habitat loss, and conflicts:

Forests especially those in the tropics serve as storehouses of biodiversity, and consequently deforestation, fragmentation, and degradation destroy the biodiversity as a whole and habitat for migratory species including the endangered ones, some of which have still to be cataloged.

Tropical forests support about two-thirds of all known species and contain 65 % of the world's 10,000 endangered species (Myers and Mittermeier, 2000).

According to the WHO, about 80 percent of the world's population relies for primary health care at least partially on traditional medicine. The biodiversity loss and associated large changes in forest cover could trigger abrupt, irreversible, and harmful changes.

Another negative effect of deforestation is increasing incidents of human-animal conflicts hitting hard the success of conservation in a way alienating the people's participation in conservation.

2. Climate change:

It is essential to distinguish between microclimates, regional climate, and global climate while assessing the effects of forests on climate, especially the effect of tropical deforestation on climate.

Deforestation can change the global change of energy not only through the micrometeorological processes but also by increasing the concentration of carbon dioxide in the atmosphere (Pinker, 1980) because carbon dioxide absorbs thermal infrared radiation in the atmosphere. Moreover, deforestation can lead to an increase in the albedo of the land surface and hence affects the radiation budget of the region.

Deforestation affects wind flows, water vapor flows and absorption of solar energy thus clearly influencing local and global climate. Deforestation disrupts normal weather patterns creating hotter and drier weather thus increasing drought and desertification, crop failures, melting of the polar ice caps, coastal flooding, and displacement of major vegetation regimes.

In the dry forest zones, land degradation has become an increasingly serious problem resulting in extreme cases of

desertification (Dregne, 1983). Desertification is a consequence of extremes in climatic variation and unsustainable land use practices including overcutting of forest cover.

Global warming or global change includes anthropogenically produced climatic and ecological problems such as recent apparent climatic temperature shifts and precipitation regimes in some areas, sea level rise, stratospheric ozone depletion, atmospheric pollution, and forest decline.

Tropical forests are *shrinking at a rate of about five percent per decade as forests are logged and cleared to supply local, regional, national, and global markets* for wood products, cattle, agricultural produce, and biofuels.

Deforestation contributes to global warming which occurs from increased atmospheric concentrations of greenhouse gases (GHG) leading to the net increase in the global mean temperature as the forests are a primary terrestrial sink of carbon.

Thus, deforestation disrupts the global carbon cycle increasing the concentration of atmospheric carbon dioxide. Tropical deforestation is responsible for the emission of roughly two billion tonnes of carbon (CO2) into the atmosphere per year (Houghton, 2005).

3. Water and soil resources loss and flooding:

Deforestation also disrupts the global water cycle. Water resources affected by deforestation include drinking water, fisheries, and aquatic habitats, flood/drought control, waterways and dams affected by siltation, less appealing water-related recreation, and damage to crops and irrigation systems from erosion and turbidity (Anon., 1994a; Bruijnzeel et al., 2005).

Deforestation also results in watersheds that are no longer able to sustain and regulate water flows from rivers and streams. Once they are gone, too much water can result in downstream flooding, many of which have caused disasters in many parts of the world.

The long-term effect of deforestation on the soil resource can be severe. Clearing the vegetative cover for slash-and-burn farming exposes the soil to the intensity of the tropical sun and torrential rains.

Forest floors with their leaf litter and porous soils easily accommodate intense rainfall. The effects of deforestation on water availability, flash floods, and dry season flows depend on what happens to these countervailing influences of infiltration and evapotranspiration- the sponge versus the fountain (Bruijnzeel, 2004).

4. Economic losses:

The tropical forests destroyed each year amount to a loss in forest capital valued at US $ 45 billion (Hansen, 997). By destroying the forests, all potential future revenues and future employment that could be derived from their sustainable management for timber and nontimber products disappear.

5. Social Consequences:

Deforestation, in other words, is an expression of social injustice. The social consequences of deforestation are many, often with devastating long-term impacts. For indigenous communities, the arrival of civilization usually means the destruction/change of their traditional lifestyle and the breakdown of their social institutions mostly with their displacement from their ancestral area.

The most immediate social impact of deforestation occurs at the local level with the loss of ecological services provided by the forests. Forests afford humans valuable services such as erosion prevention, flood control, water treatment, fisheries protection, and pollination functions that are particularly important to the world's poorest people who rely on natural resources for their everyday survival. By destroying the forests, we risk the quality of life, gamble with the stability of climate and local weather, threaten the existence of other species, and undermine the valuable services provided by biological diversity.

Chapter 9: Key Takeaways

1. Deforestation has multifaceted effects, including biodiversity loss, habitat destruction, and human-animal conflicts. It contributes to climate change by altering energy balance and increasing carbon dioxide levels, impacting weather patterns and leading to desertification.

2. Loss of forests disrupts water cycles, causing floods, soil erosion, and water scarcity, affecting agriculture and urban water sources. Economically, it results in significant capital loss and social injustice, displacing indigenous communities and disrupting traditional lifestyles. Deforestation jeopardizes ecological services vital for human survival, highlighting the urgent need for sustainable forest management.

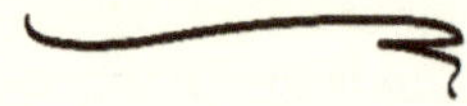

Chapter 10: Strategic Plan to Reduce Deforestation

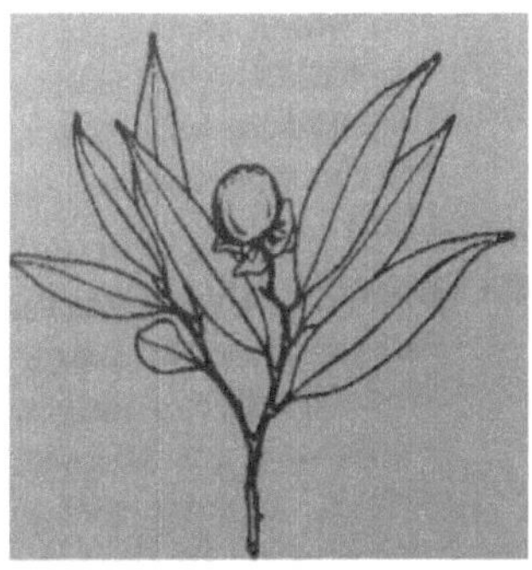

There are no general solutions and strategies since these will vary with region and will change over time. The strategies should be such that on one hand, they should recognize the critical roles of national, state, and municipal/local governments. On the other hand, they should empower civil society and the private sector to take a proactive role in reducing deforestation, often working in conjunction with the government.

1. Reduce population growth and increase per capita incomes:

Reduction of population growth is pivotal in reducing deforestation in the developing countries. Consequent to reduced population, an increase in per capita income will occur as a consequence of increased incomes and literacy rates which will reduce pressure on the remaining forests for new human settlement and land use change.

2. Reducing emissions from deforestation and forest degradation (REDD):

Many international organizations including the United Nations and the World Bank have begun to develop programs to curb deforestation mainly through Reducing Emissions from Deforestation and Forest Degradation (REDD) which uses direct monetary or other incentives to encourage developing countries to limit and/or roll back deforestation.

Significant work is underway on tools for use in monitoring developing countries' adherence to their agreed REDDS targets.

3. Increase the area and standard of management of protected areas:

The provision of protected areas is fundamental in any attempt to conserve biodiversity. Protected areas alone, however, are not sufficient to conserve biodiversity. They should be considered alongside and as part of, a wider strategy to conserve biodiversity.

The minimum area of forest to be protected is generally considered to be 10 percent of the total forest area. It is reported that 12.4 percent of the world's forests are located within protected areas. Tropical and temperate forests have the highest proportions of their forests in protected areas and boreal forests have the least. The Americas have the maximum proportion while Europe has the minimum proportion of protected areas.

4. Increase the area of forest permanently reserved for timber production:

If the forest does not have a dedicated long-term tenure for timber production, then there is no incentive to care for the long-term interests of the forest. *FAO (2001) found that 89 percent of forests in industrialized countries were under some form of management but only about 6 percent were in developing countries.*

If **20 percent could be set aside**, not only could timber demand be sustainably met but buffer zones could be established to consolidate the protected areas. This would form a conservation estate that would be one of the largest and most important in the world (Anon., 2001a).

5. Increase the perceived and actual value of forests:

There are several ways of achieving increasing the perceived and actual value of forests. Governments can impose realistic prices on stumpage and forest rent and can invest in improving the sustainable productivity of the forest. National and international beneficiaries of the environmental services of forests have to pay for such services (Chomitz et al., 2007).

There has been some success in devising schemes to collect payments for environmental services like carbon sequestration, biodiversity conservation, catchment protection, and www.intechopen.com. This success can further be realized by integrating a participatory mode of management with these collection schemes to ensure rights and tenure with equity in resource and benefit sharing for improving the livelihood of the rural poor who are the primary stakeholders of conservation and management.

6. Promote sustainable management

To promote sustainable forest management, it must be sustainable ecologically, economically, and socially. Achieving ecological sustainability means that silviculture and management should not reduce biodiversity, soil erosion should be controlled, soil fertility should not be lost, water quality on and off-site should be maintained and forest health and vitality should be safeguarded.

However, management for environmental services alone is not economically and socially sustainable. It will not happen until or unless the developing nations have reached a stage of development and affluence that they can accommodate the costs of doing so.

Alternatively, the developed world must be prepared to meet all the costs (Chomitz et al., 2007; Anon., 2010; 2011). There are vast areas of unused land some of which are degraded and of low fertility. *Technological advances are being made to bring this land back into production.* This should be a major priority since a significant proportion of cleared tropical forests will eventually end up as degraded land of low fertility.

7. Encouraging substitutes:

For all purposes where tropical or other timber is used, other woods or materials could be substituted. We can stop using timber and urge others to do the same. **As long as there is a market for wood products, trees will continue to be cut down**. Labeling schemes, aimed at helping consumers to choose environmentally friendly timbers are currently being discussed in many countries.

8. Increase the area of forest plantation:

Increasing the area of forest plantations by using vacant or unused lands and waste and marginal lands, especially as roadside, along railway tracts, on contours, avenues, boundaries, and on land not suited for agricultural production should have a net positive benefit. Planting trees outside forest areas will reduce pressure on forests for timber, fodder, and fuelwood demands. Moreover, the deforested areas need to be reforested.

9 Strengthen government and non-government institutions and policies:

A strong and stable government is essential to slow down the rate of deforestation. FAO (2010) considered that half of the current tropical deforestation could be stopped if the governments of deforesting countries were determined to do so (Anon., 2010).

Environmental NGOs' contribution to conservation management has been enormous. They have the advantage over government organizations and large international organizations because they are not constrained by government-government bureaucracy and inertia. They are better equipped to bypass corruption and they are very effective at getting to the people at the frontier who are in most need.

10. Participatory Forest management and rights:

For forest management to succeed at the forest frontier, all parties with an interest in the fate of the forest should be communally involved in planning, management, and profit sharing.

The balance of rights can be tilted strongly toward society in the form of publicly owned strictly protected areas. State ownership and management can be retained but with sustainable timber extraction allowed.

As of now much of the world's tropical forests are state but community participation in forest ownership and management needs to be encouraged with restrictions on extraction and conversion. Land reform is essential to address the problem of deforestation.

Therefore, the recognition of traditional laws of the Indigenous peoples as Indigenous rights will address the conflicts between customary and statutory laws and regulations related to forest ownership and natural resource use while ensuring the conservation of forest resources by the indigenous communities.

A means must be found to reconcile conservation and development by involving local/indigenous populations more closely in the decision-making process and by taking the interactions between 'societies and forest resources more fully into account.

11. Support and reforms:

Aid organizations like the World Bank have traditionally favored spectacular large-scale developmental projects. In all cases when such projects are proposed there has been a massive opposition from local people.

Campaigns opposing such developments and the campaigns to reform the large aid agencies that fund such schemes should be supported. Local campaigns against specific mining, dams, and industrial, and tourist developments should be supported. Further reform of the World Bank and other such organizations is largely the demand of time.

12. Increase investment in research, education, and extension:

Training and education of stakeholders help people understand how to prevent and reduce adverse environmental effects associated with deforestation and forestry activities and take appropriate action when possible. Research substantiates it and helps to understand the problem, its cause, and mitigation.

This arena is lagging in the paucity of funds and investments to encourage this arena. There is a lack of knowledge and information in the general community about forests and forestry. Forest managers and those developing forest policies need to be comprehensively educated and need to appreciate the complexity of the interacting ecological, economic, social, cultural, and political factors involved.

13. Improve the information base and monitoring:

Information on the global distribution of biodiversity and forest poverty is inadequate. Knowledge of how much forest, where it is, and what it is composed of seems to be straightforward but surprisingly this most basic information is not always available.

The international community could undertake monitoring efforts that would have immediate payoffs. A priority is to fund and coordinate basic monitoring of the rate, location, and causes of global deforestation and forest poverty along with the impacts of project and policy interventions. Without this information, policymakers are flying blind and interest groups lack a solid basis for dialogue (Chomitz et al., 2007).

14. Policy, legislative, and regulatory measures-enforcement and compliance:

A wide variety of policy statements and legislative and regulatory measures have been established to protect forests but need to be effectively enforced.

Laws, policies, and legislation should be such that they encourage local people and institutional participation in forestry management and conservation along with safeguarding indigenous people's traditional rights and tenure with rightful sharing of benefits. Many formal and informal enforcement/compliance mechanisms are used to prevent deforestation and environmental problems from forestry activities.

Conclusion: Economic globalization combined with the looming global land scarcity increases the complexity of future pathways of land use change. In a more interconnected world, agricultural intensification may cause more rather than less cropland expansion.

The apparent trade-off between forest and agriculture can be minimized through spatial management and the use of degraded or low-competition lands. This can be further addressed by community-based forest management which builds on political goodwill and strong community institutions. New challenges from climate change require urgent action to explore and protect the local value of forests for livelihood even more.

This is particularly true in the case of emerging activities undertaken as part of REDD+ activities where broad forest governance is aligned with it along with people's participation ensuring livelihood benefits of the people dependent on forests. These renewed activities will safeguard traditional ways of life and the environmentally important forest ecosystems of the world.

Chapter 10: Key Takeaways

1. **Population Control and Income Growth**: Emphasizes the importance of reducing population growth and increasing per capita income to alleviate pressure on forests. Similarly, many other strategies like REDD Programs, Protected Areas, and Sustainable
2. **Management, Timber Production Reserves,** Increasing Forest Value, Promoting Sustainable

Management, Encouraging Substitutes and Plantations, Strengthening Institutions and Policies, Supporting Reforms and Investments, Improving Information and Monitoring, Policy Enforcement and Compliance,

In conclusion, there is the urgency of addressing deforestation through a combination of economic, social, and environmental strategies while involving local communities and ensuring sustainable forest management practices.

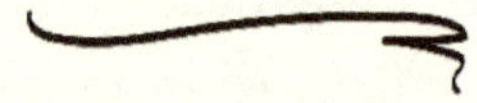

PART -V: HUMANITY NEEDS THE WISDOM TO ADDRESS THE UNHEARD CRY OF PLANTS AND FORESTS - THE LIFELINE OF SURVIVAL OF ALL LIVING BEINGS

Chapter 11: To address the Unheard Cry of Plants and Forests, humanity needs Mass Movements at all Levels of Society

It's disheartening to witness the ongoing assaults on our planet's plants and forests, especially considering their vital role in sustaining life on Earth.   The suffering of Plants and their habitats - the Forests, happens every day, particularly in the tropics due to various factors, both natural and anthropogenic (human-induced).

Deforestation is the most significant cause of this suffering for plants and forests. Deforestation is the conversion of forest to an alternative permanent non-forested land use such as agriculture, logging grazing, urbanization, and infrastructure development.   Deforestation is primarily a concern for the developing countries of the tropics as it is shrinking areas of the tropical forests causing loss of biodiversity and enhancing the greenhouse effect.

A detailed analytical discussion about deforestation and its effects on plants and forests has already been done under Chapter -7.

Besides, Forest degradation with other factors like Climate Change - Rising temperatures, and extreme weather events threaten plant life and habitats; Pollution- Industrial and urban pollution harms plant health and ecosystem vitality; Invasive Species- Introduced plants compete with natives, altering ecosystems; Forest Fragmentation - Development isolates plant populations, disrupting ecological processes.

Furthermore, Humanity's lack of awareness, static aversion to change, and failure to fully recognize the urgency of the situation contribute to the suffering of plants and forests. Unawareness leads to harmful actions like habitat destruction and pollution. A reluctance to change entrenched behaviors impedes efforts to mitigate this suffering. Addressing these barriers requires raising awareness, fostering empathy, and promoting stewardship. Despite efforts, the **"unheard cry"** persists due to competing priorities and short-term gains without the vision of posterity.

Thirty percent of the earth's land area or about 3.9 billion hectares is covered by forests. It was estimated that the original forest cover was approximately six billion hectares.

Indeed, addressing the unheard cry of plants and forests necessitates a mass movement and multi-faceted approach that engages stakeholders at all levels of society from local communities to national governments and international organizations towards protecting plants and forests for present and future generations.

Mass movements play a crucial role in protecting plants and forests by mobilizing large numbers of people to advocate for conservation and take action to preserve these ecosystems.

Increasing public awareness about the importance of plants and forests is essential. Mass movements have the power to raise awareness on a large scale. By organizing rallies, marches, and public campaigns, mass movements can educate people about the importance of plants and forests and the threats they face, such as deforestation, habitat destruction, and climate change. Educational campaigns, documentaries, and social media initiatives can help people understand the vital role these ecosystems play in maintaining biodiversity, regulating the climate, and providing essential resources.

Overall, mass movements play a crucial role in protecting plants and forests by raising awareness, exerting political pressure, engaging communities, taking direct action, advocating for policy change, and fostering global solidarity. By harnessing the collective power of people united in their commitment to conservation, mass movements can help safeguard these essential ecosystems for future generations.

Here are some essential components.

1. Local Communities:

Local communities are often the custodians of forests and have invaluable traditional knowledge about plant and forest ecosystems. They can actively participate in conservation efforts through sustainable land management practices, reforestation initiatives, and community-based natural resource management programs.

Supporting and participating in conservation projects aimed at preserving plant species and restoring degraded forests is critical. This can involve activities such as tree planting, habitat restoration, and the establishment of protected areas.

Empowering local communities to manage and protect their forests can lead to more effective and sustainable conservation outcomes by

- Implementing community-based conservation projects that engage local stakeholders, including indigenous communities and forest-dependent populations.

- Promoting sustainable land management practices such as agroforestry and rotational grazing to reduce pressure on forested areas.

- Establishing and enforcing protected areas and reserves to safeguard critical ecosystems and biodiversity hotspots.

2. National Governments and Policymakers:

National and local governments play a crucial role in enacting and enforcing policies and regulations that protect plant and forest ecosystems.

They can develop land use planning strategies that prioritize conservation and sustainable management, allocate resources for protected area management, and strengthen law enforcement to combat illegal logging and land encroachment.

Advocating for stronger environmental regulations and policies to protect plants and forests is necessary. This includes advocating for sustainable land-use practices, stricter regulations on deforestation and logging, and promoting renewable energy sources to reduce reliance on fossil fuels.

Promote sustainable land use planning and management practices that prioritize the conservation of biodiversity and ecosystem services, including the protection of critical habitats and the establishment of ecological corridors.

Governments can also support initiatives that promote sustainable livelihoods for forest-dependent communities and provide incentives for private landowners to engage in conservation practices by

- Enacting and enforcing laws to regulate deforestation, illegal logging, and land conversion for agriculture or urban development.

- Implementing sustainable forestry practices and certification schemes to ensure the responsible management of forest resources.

- Investing in reforestation and afforestation programs to restore degraded landscapes and expand forest cover.

3. International Organizations and Global Cooperation:

International organizations, such as the United Nations Environment Programme (UNEP) and the World Bank, provide funding, technical assistance, and policy guidance to support global conservation efforts.

They can facilitate cooperation among countries, promote knowledge exchange, and coordinate international initiatives to address cross-border challenges such as deforestation and climate change.

Donors and philanthropic organizations can contribute financial resources to support conservation projects, capacity building, and research initiatives aimed at protecting plants and forests worldwide.

By mobilizing the collective efforts of these diverse stakeholders and implementing coordinated actions at local, national, and global levels, we can effectively address the unheard cry of plants and forests and ensure their long-term survival for the benefit of present and future generations.

- Strengthening international agreements and frameworks for forest conservation, such as the United Nations Framework Convention on Climate Change (UNFCCC) and the Convention on Biological Diversity (CBD).

- Supporting initiatives like REDD+ (Reducing Emissions from Deforestation and Forest Degradation) that incentivize forest conservation and sustainable land use practices in developing countries.

- Mobilizing financial resources and technical assistance to support forest conservation and sustainable development efforts in regions facing the greatest threats.

4. Scientific Community, Research, & Monitoring:

Investing in research and innovation to develop new technologies and practices that promote plant and forest conservation is crucial. This includes research on plant genetics, sustainable forestry techniques, and innovative solutions for mitigating the impacts of climate change on forest ecosystems.

Scientists and researchers contribute essential knowledge and expertise to understanding the ecological processes that sustain plant and forest ecosystems. They can research topics such as biodiversity conservation, ecosystem restoration, and the impacts of climate change on plants and forests.

Collaborative research efforts can inform evidence-based conservation strategies and facilitate the development of innovative solutions to address the challenges facing plants and forests by

- Conducting scientific research to better understand the ecological, economic, and social dynamics of forests and their role in mitigating climate change.

- Monitoring forest cover and biodiversity using satellite imagery, remote sensing technologies, and on-the-ground surveys to track changes over time and inform conservation strategies.

- Sharing knowledge and best practices through networks and partnerships to improve conservation outcomes and build capacity at all levels.

5. Education and Awareness:

Implement comprehensive environmental education programs in schools and communities to raise awareness about the importance of plants and forests, their ecological functions, and the threats they face.

Utilize various media platforms, including social media, documentaries, and public campaigns, to disseminate information and foster public engagement on issues related to plant and forest conservation by

- Raising awareness about the importance of forests and biodiversity through education, outreach, and advocacy efforts.

- Promoting sustainable consumer choices and supporting businesses that prioritize forest-friendly products and practices.

- Empowering local communities and indigenous peoples to participate in decision-making processes and stewardship of forest resources.

6. Non-Governmental Organizations (NGOs):

NGOs play a vital role in raising awareness, advocating for policy change, and implementing on-the-ground conservation projects.

They can mobilize resources, provide technical assistance to local communities, and engage in advocacy campaigns to promote plant and forest conservation.

NGOs often work in partnership with governments, local communities, and other stakeholders to implement integrated conservation approaches that address both environmental and socio-economic concerns.

7. Businesses and Industries:

Businesses have a responsibility to minimize their environmental footprint and mitigate the impacts of their operations on plants and forests.

They can adopt sustainable sourcing practices, support certification schemes for responsibly sourced forest products, and invest in conservation initiatives as part of their corporate social responsibility commitments.

Collaboration between businesses, NGOs, and governments can drive the adoption of sustainable practices throughout supply chains and promote the conservation of plant and forest ecosystems.

8. Consumer Choices:

Making environmentally conscious consumer choices can also make a difference. Supporting sustainable forestry practices, purchasing products from companies committed to ethical sourcing, and reducing consumption of goods that contribute to deforestation can help reduce the demand for products that harm plant and forest ecosystems.

By actively participating in movements focused on plant and forest conservation, humanity can work together to protect these silent sufferers and ensure a healthier and more sustainable future for our planet.

9. Financial Incentives and Support:

Provide financial incentives, grants, and technical assistance to landowners, farmers, and forest-dependent communities to adopt sustainable land management practices and participate in conservation efforts.

Explore innovative financing mechanisms, such as payments for ecosystem services (PES) and biodiversity offsets, to incentivize forest conservation and restoration activities.

By taking these steps collectively and collaboratively, we can work towards addressing the unheard cry of plants and forests and securing a more sustainable future for all life on Earth.

10. We all want Development- a true development for every citizen of this mother earth -but not at the cost of plants and forests:

Of late without appreciating the benefit for more people for longer periods, we humans oft for quick, shortcut methods by clearing the age-old pristine forest in the name of development. As a result, we lose the healthy living Ecosystem of our surroundings by destroying the entire Air, Water, Soil, and oxygen-producing factories, i.e., the plants and Forests. We must and should, praise the naturally gifted forests and protect them with all humility and honor.

We need a ban on tree felling worldwide irrespective of ownership of land. More than forming stringent policies, we need to facilitate mass movement creating more awareness for the protection, conservation, and augmentation of more plants and Forests.

More awakening needs to be built up among the people, students, planners, etc. so that everyone starts growing plants of their own for the amount of O2 he/she consumes every day. It does not logically support that we consume a large quantity of a resource, that we never produce, nor pay for the consumption of this, nor even think for its protection!

Every citizen of this planet needs to live with good health and prosperity, not at the cost of any other living beings particularly those who help us in our daily lives with basic life-supporting systems. The plants and their habitats- the forests provide us with all these prime resources for humans and also other living beings. *So we do not exploit and destroy these living species with life forms like us- the plants in the name of development. We love them and protect them creating awareness among all sections of humanities.*

Hence, there must be some policies that every family must plant and protect a minimum number of plants –the oxygen-producing factories.

Finally, Public Policy for the protection of existing forests and forestland, increasing the forest cover of the country essentially needs to be framed. Further, protecting the fragile Ecosystem – restoring fresh O2 flow, promoting perennial water flow – protecting the natural water bodies, enhancing groundwater discharge raising ground water table, and ensuring sustained yield of life-saving drugs from the forest are required to be outlined in Public Policy for all countries of this beautiful planet- the Mother Earth.

Chapter-11: Key Takeaways

1. To address the unheard cry of plants and forests, mass movements at all societal levels are crucial. Deforestation, climate change, pollution, invasive species, and habitat fragmentation pose significant threats. Lack of awareness and reluctance to change exacerbates the situation.

2. Protecting these ecosystems requires a multi-faceted present approach involving local communities, governments, international organizations, the scientific community, NGOs, businesses, consumers, financial

incentives, and balancing development with conservation. These efforts aim to raise awareness, advocate for policy change, implement conservation projects, promote sustainable practices, and ensure global solidarity.

In conclusion, the article stresses the importance of collective action and policy measures to protect plants and forests for the benefit of humanity and all other living beings for the present and the generations to come.

Chapter 12: Through the Tragic History of Deforestation, Humanity finds the Wisdom to protect the lives of Plants and Forests Worldwide

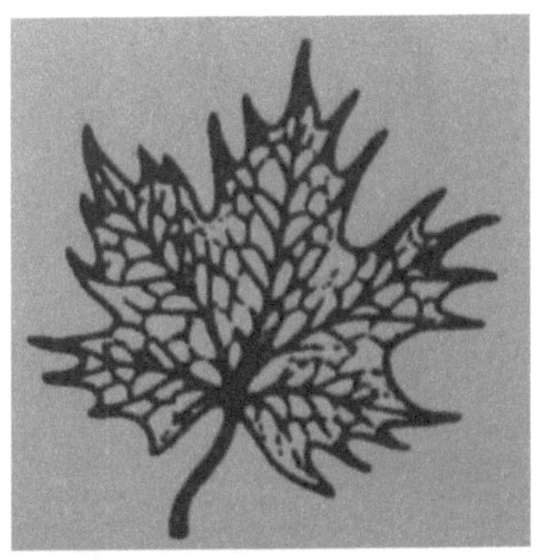

Before we look at trends in deforestation across the world specifically, it's useful to understand the net change in forest cover.

The net change in forest cover measures any gains in forest cover – either through natural forest expansion or afforestation through tree planting – minus deforestation.

The map depicted below (vide-map 11.1) shows the net change in forest cover across the world. Countries with a positive change (shown in green) are regrowing forests faster than they're losing it.

Countries with a negative change (shown in red) are losing more than they can restore.

Map- 11.1- Annual change in forest area, 2015
The net change in forest area measures forest expansion (either through afforestation or natural expansion) minus deforestation

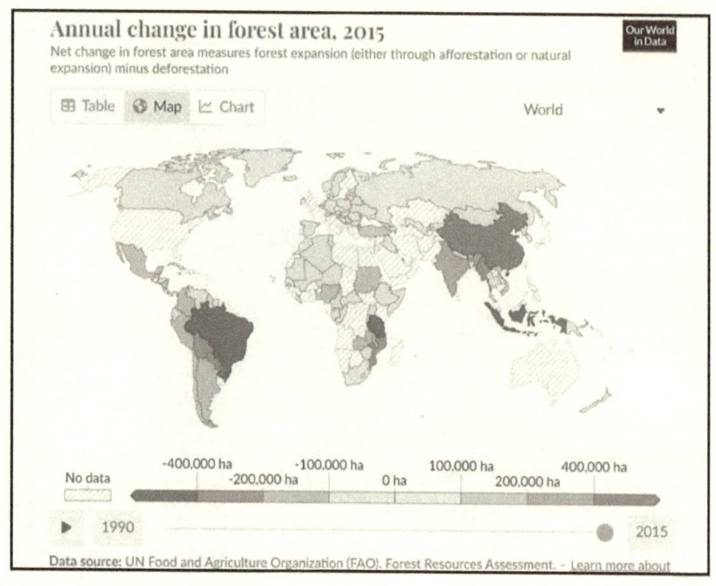

How much deforestation occurs each year?

Net forest loss is not the same as deforestation – it measures deforestation plus any gains in forest over a given period. Over the decade since 2010, the net loss in forests globally was 4.7 million hectares per year.1 However, deforestation rates were significantly higher.

Global forests: In the visualization, we see the breakdown of global land area. (vide Figure 11.1)

10% of the world is covered by glaciers, and a further 19% is barren land – (deserts, dry salt flats, beaches, dunes, and exposed rocks). This leaves what we call 'habitable land'(76%). Forests account for a little over one-third (38%) of habitable land area. This is around one-quarter (26%) of the total (both habitable and uninhabitable) land area.

Figure-11.1-Chart showing the breakdown of global land area

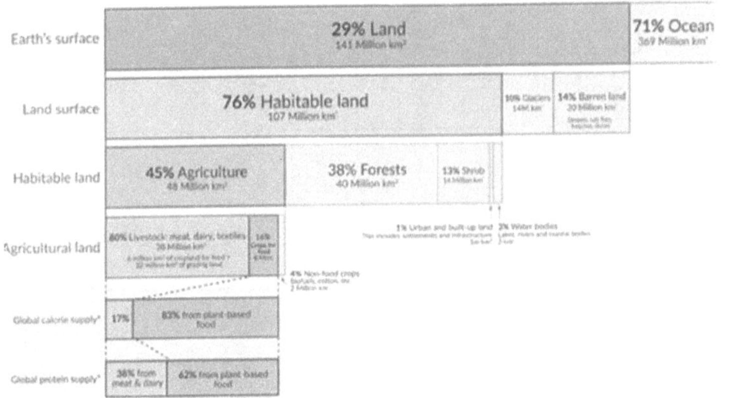

How much forest has the world lost? When in history did, we lose it?

In the chart, we see how the cover of the earth's surface has changed over the past 10,000 years. This is shortly after the end of the last great ice age, through to the present day.2

The bar chart just below shows the earth's surface cover just after the end of the last ice age.3

Figure-11.2 - Chart showing that Humanity destroyed one-third of the world's forests by expanding Agricultural Land

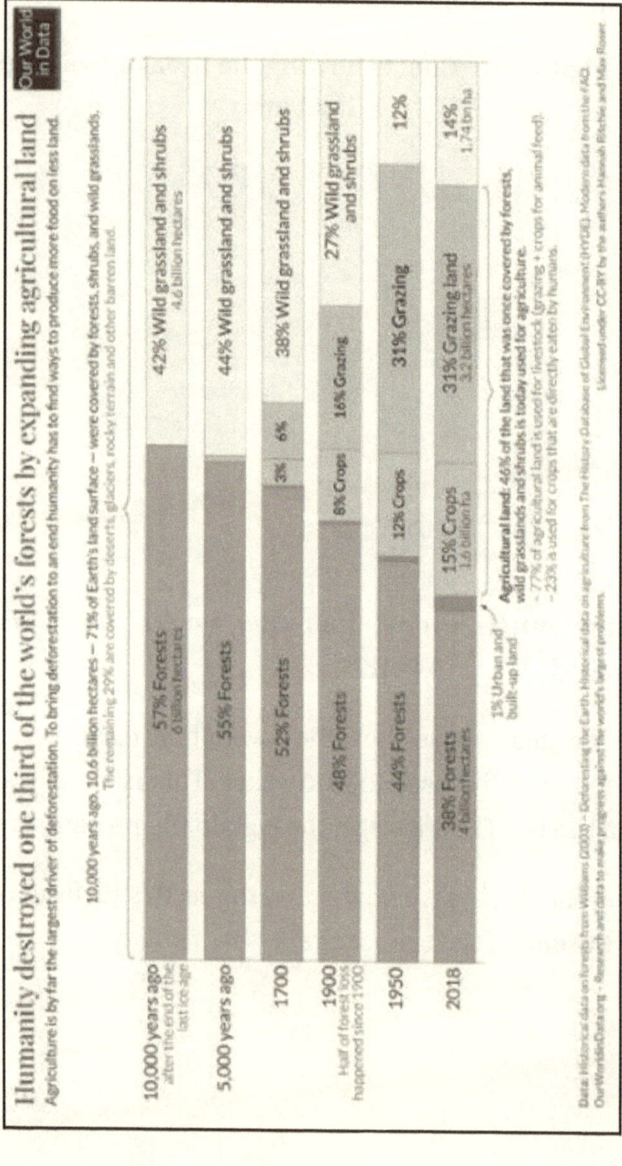

i). Let's start at the top of the chart. We see that of the 14.9 billion hectares of land on the planet, only 71% of it is habitable – the other 29% is barren land such as deserts, salt flats, dunes, or glaciers.

ii).10,000 years ago 57% of the world's habitable land was covered by forest. That was 6 billion hectares. Today, only 4 billion hectares are left. The world has lost one-third of its forest.

iii). Only 10% of this was lost in the first half of this period, until 5,000 years ago. The global population at this time was small and growing very slowly – there were fewer than 50 million people in the world. The amount of land per person that was needed to produce enough food was much larger than today. There was little pressure on forests as the global population was small.

iv). If we fast-forward to 1700AD when the global population had increased more than ten-fold, to 603 million. The amount of land used for agriculture – land to grow crops as well as grazing land for livestock – was expanding. We can notice other land uses such as wild grasslands and shrubbery in the chart. Still, more than half of the world's habitable land was forested.

v). The turn of the 20th century is when global forest loss reached the halfway point: half of total forest loss occurred from 8,000 BC to 1900AD;

vi). The other half occurred in the last century alone. This emphasizes two important points.

First, Deforestation isn't a recent issue; even with smaller populations in the past, humans had a significant impact on forests due to agricultural needs and wood consumption for fuel.

Second, Over the last century, deforestation has accelerated dramatically, with the world losing as much forest in 100 years as it did in the previous 9,000 years. This acceleration is mainly attributed to the expansion of agricultural land rather than urbanization.

How can we put an end to our long history of deforestation?

This might paint a bleak picture for the future of the world's forests: the United Nations projects that the global population will continue to grow, reaching 10.8 billion by 2100. But there are real reasons to believe that this century doesn't have to replicate the destruction of the last one.

The world passed 'peaked deforestation' in the 1980s and it has been on the decline since then – we take a look at rates of forest loss since 1700AD. Improvements in crop yields mean the per capita demand for agricultural land continues to fall.

Figure-11.2-Agricultural land per capita: Agricultural land is the sum of cropland and land used as pasture for grazing livestock.

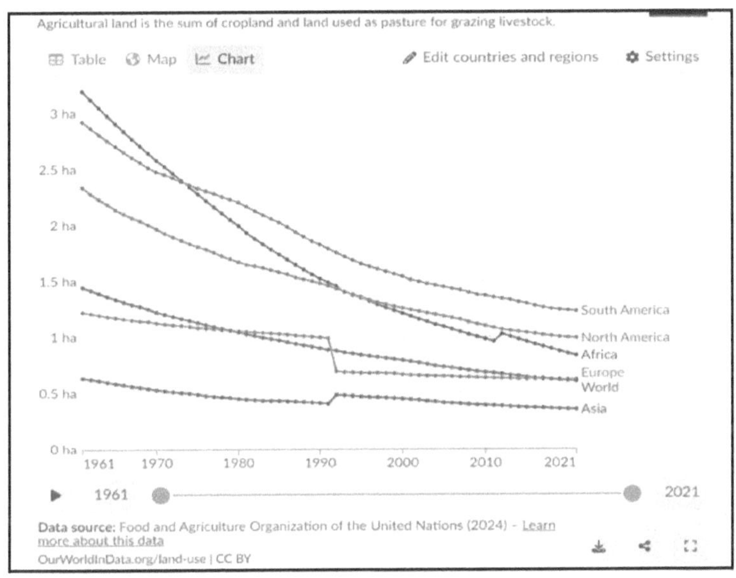

We see this in the chart. Since 1961, the amount of land we use for agriculture increased by only 7%. Meanwhile, the global population increased by 147% – from 3.1 to 7.6 billion.4 This means that agricultural land per person is more than halved, from 1.45 to 0.63 hectares.

With the growth of technological innovations such as lab-grown meat and substitute products, there is the real possibility that we can continue to enjoy meat or meat-like foods while freeing up the massive amounts of land we use to raise livestock.

If we can take advantage of these innovations, we can bring deforestation to an end. A future with more people and more forests is possible.

Global deforestation peaked in the 1980s, Can we bring it to an end?

Since the end of the last great ice age – 10,000 years ago – the world has lost one-third of its forests.5 Two billion hectares of forest – have been cleared to grow crops, raise livestock, and use for fuelwood.

Humans have been cutting down trees for millennia but the rate of forest loss accelerated rapidly in the last few centuries. *Half of the global forest loss occurred between 8,000 BC and 1900AD; the other half was lost in the last century alone.*

To understand this more recent loss of forest, let's zoom in on the last 300 years. The world lost 1.5 billion hectares of forest over that period.

In the chart, we see the decadal losses and gains in global forest cover. **On the horizontal axis, we have time, spanning from 1700 to 2020; on the vertical axis, we have the decadal change in forest cover. The taller the bar, the larger the change in forest area. This is measured in hectares, which is equivalent to 10,000 m² (Vide Figure 11.3).**

Forest loss measures the net change in forest cover: the loss in forests due to deforestation plus any expansion of forest through afforestation.

Regrettably, there is no single source that provides consistent and transparent data on deforestation rates over this period. This means we have had to use two separate datasets to show this change over time.

Figure -11.3- Decadal losses in global forest over the last three centuries

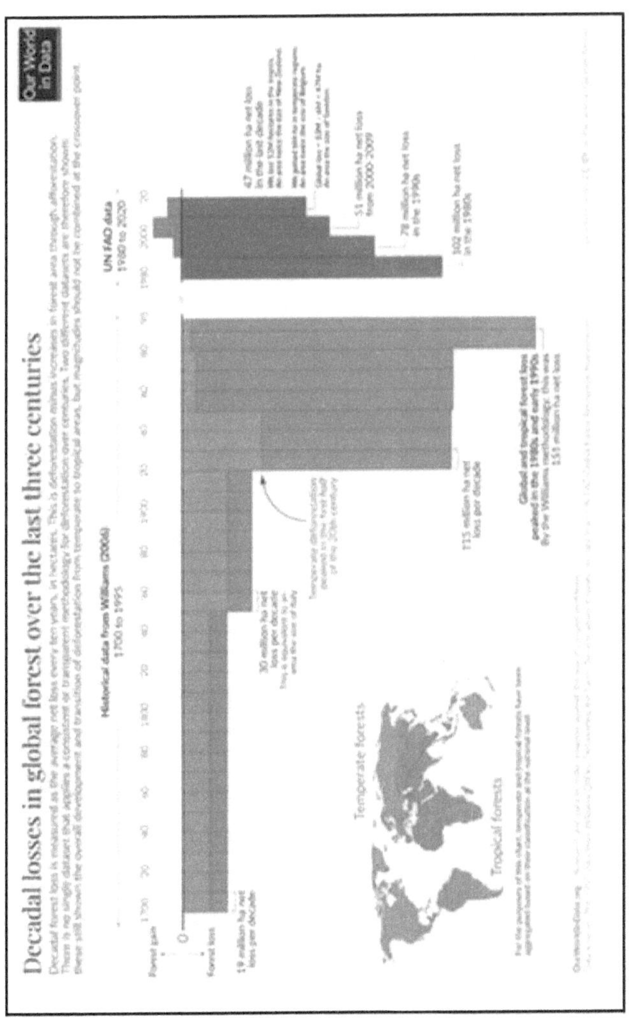

The first series of data comes from Williams (2006), who estimates deforestation rates from 1700 to 1995.[7] Due to poor data resolution, these are often given as average rates over longer periods.

The second series comes from the UN Food and Agriculture Organization (FAO). It produces a new assessment of global forests every 5 years.

From 1700 to 1850, 19 million hectares of forest were cleared every decade, mainly in temperate regions like Europe and North America for agriculture, and wood for energy, and construction.

In the 20th century, deforestation rates accelerated, especially in tropical regions of Asia and Latin America, peaking in the 1980s.

Interestingly, the UN FAO 1990 report also estimated that deforestation in tropical 'developing' countries was 154 million hectares. However, it estimated that the regrowth of old forests offset some of these losses, leading to a net loss of 102 million hectares.

The latest UN Forest Resources Assessment estimates that the net loss in forests has declined in the last three decades, from 78 million hectares in the 1990s to 47 million hectares in the 2010s.[11] This data maps an expected pathway based on what we know from how human-forest interactions evolve. However, recent data suggests a decline in net forest loss, with some countries transitioning to regrowth phases.

That is what has happened in temperate regions: they have gone through a period of high deforestation rates, before a slowing and reversal of this trend. Despite progress, deforestation remains a significant threat, particularly in biodiversity-rich tropical regions.

Forest recovery and plantation efforts offset some deforestation, but it's not a complete solution. Many countries have successfully ended deforestation and achieved reforestation, indicating a positive future is possible.

There is some progress, but it needs to happen much faster. The world is still losing large amounts of primary forests every year. To put these numbers in context: during the 1990s and first decade of the 2000s, an area almost the size of India was deforested.[12] Even with the 'improved' rates in the 2010s, this still amounted to an area around twice the size of Spain.[13]

The regrowth of forests is a positive development. In the chart below, (Vide Figure 11.4) we see how this affects the net change in global forests. Forest recovery and plantation 'offsets' a lot of deforestation such that the net losses are around half the rates of deforestation alone.

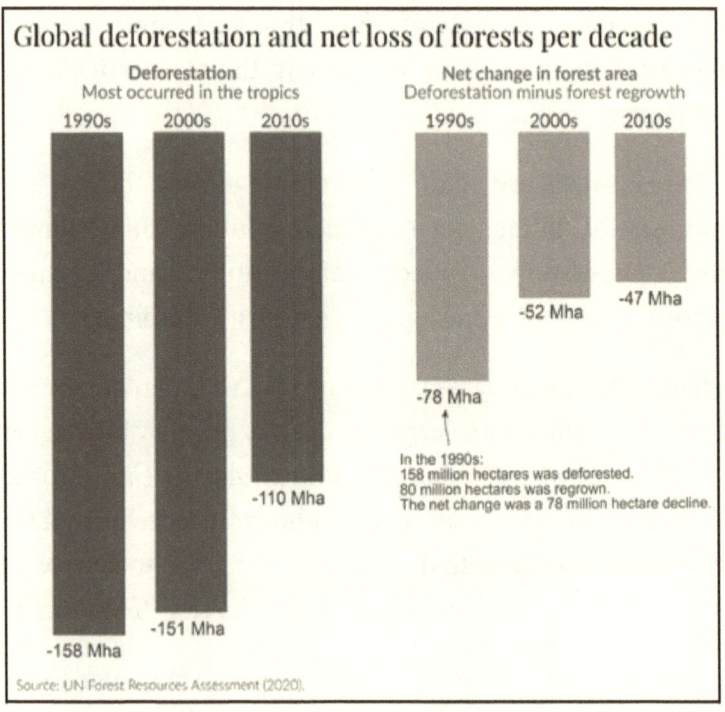

But we should be cautious here: it's often not the case that the 'positives' of regrowing one hectare of forest offset the 'losses' of one hectare of deforestation. Cutting down one hectare of rich, tropical rainforest cannot be completely offset by the plantation of forest in a temperate country. Forest expansion is positive, but does not negate the need to finally end deforestation.

The history of deforestation is a tragic one, in which we have not only these wild and beautiful landscapes but also the wildlife within them. But the fact that forest transitions are possible should give us confidence that a positive future is possible. Many countries have not only ended deforestation but achieved substantial reforestation. **It will be possible for our generation to achieve the same on a global scale and bring the 10,000-year history of forest loss to an end.**

If we want to end deforestation we need to understand where and why it's happening; where countries are within their transition; and what can be done to accelerate their progress through it. We need to pass the transition point as soon as possible while minimizing the amount of forest we lose along the way.

Chapter 12: Key Takeaways

1. Humanity has a long history of deforestation, losing one-third of the world's forests over the past 10,000 years. Accelerated deforestation began in the last few centuries, particularly in the 20th century, due to agricultural expansion.

2. Since the 1980s, global deforestation has been declining, with improvements in agricultural efficiency. Recent data shows a decrease in net forest loss, indicating some countries are transitioning to forest regrowth phases. While forest recovery efforts offset some deforestation, it's not enough to fully address the problem. Ending deforestation requires understanding its causes and accelerating transition efforts worldwide.

3. Despite challenges, there's hope for a positive future
   with increased forest conservation and restoration
   efforts by all sections of human society for the plants
   and forests- the lifeline of survival of all living beings on
   the planet Earth.

REFERENCES

1. FAO. 2020. Global Forest Resources Assessment 2020 – Key findings. Rome. https://doi.org/10.4060/ca8753en

2. The data used in this chart comes from several sources.

Forests – this data is primarily sourced from the UN Food and Agriculture Organization (FAO). .... rates from Williams (2003) to document forest change over the last 300 years – this gives us data on forest change from 1700 onwards.

The definition of 'forest' can vary depending on aspects such as tree density and height....... a one-third loss.

Agricultural and urban land – The UN FAO Statistical database provides data...... sourced from the work of Ellis et al. (2020).

FAO and UNEP. 2020. The State of the World's Forests 2020. Forests, biodiversity, and people. Rome.

Williams, M. (2003). Deforesting the earth: from prehistory to global crisis. University of Chicago Press.

Ellis, E. C., Beusen, A. H., & Goldewijk, K. K. (2020). Anthropogenic Biomes: 10,000 BCE to 2015 CE. Land, 9(5), 129.

3. Estimates vary, but most date the end of the last great ice age to around 11,700 years ago.Kump, L. R., Kasting, J. F., &

Crane, R. G. (2004). The Earth System (Vol. 432). Upper Saddle River, NJ: Pearson Prentice Hall.

4. We can calculate this increase as [(7.63 billion - 3.09 billion) / 3.09 billion * 100 = 147%].

5. Estimates vary, but most date the end of the last great ice age to around 11,700 years ago.

Kump, L. R., Kasting, J. F., & Crane, R. G. (2004). The Earth System (Vol. 432). Upper Saddle River, NJ: Pearson Prentice Hall.

6. Year-to-year data on forest change comes with several issues: – including the UN Food and Agriculture Organization – tend decadal periods.

7. Williams, M. (2003). Deforesting the earth: from prehistory to global crisis. University of Chicago Press.

8. The data for 1990 to 2000 is from the latest assessment: the UN's Global Forest Resources Assessment 2020.

FAO (2020). Global Forest Resources Assessment 2020: Main report. Rome. https://doi.org/10.4060/ca9825en.

9. Mather, A. S., Fairbairn, J., & Needle, C. L. (1999). The course and drivers of the forest transition: the case of France. Journal of Rural Studies, 15(1), 65-90.

Mather, A. S., & Needle, C. L. (2000). The relationships of population and forest trends. Geographical Journal, 166(1), 2-13.

10. It estimated that the net change in forests without plantations was 121 million hectares. With plantations included – as is standard for the UN's forest assessments – this was 102 million hectares.

11. Hosonuma, N., Herold, M., De Sy, V., De Fries, R. S., Brockhaus, M., Verchot, L., ... & Romijn, E. (2012). An assessment of deforestation and forest degradation drivers in developing countries. Environmental Research Letters, 7(4), 044009.

12. The area of India is around 330 million hectares. The combined losses in the 1990s and 2000s were 309 million hectares. Just 6% less than the size of India.

13. The area of Spain is around 51 million hectares. Double this area is around 102 million hectares – a little under 110 million hectares.

14. Shivanna KR. The Sixth Mass Extinction Crisis and its Impact on Biodiversity and Human Welfare. Resonance. 2020; 25:93–109. doi: 10.1007/s12045-019-0924-z. [CrossRef] [Google Scholar]

15. Hazarika TK, Marak S, Mandal D, Shukla AC. Underutilized and unexploited fruits of Indo-Burma hot spot, Meghalaya, north-east India:...... 2016; 63:289–304. doi: 10.1007/s10722-015-0248-0. [CrossRef] [Google Scholar]

16. Life Movements in Plants Jagadish Chandra Bose proved that plants are like any other life form.

17. Deforestation: Causes, Effects and Control Strategies: Sumit Chakravarty1, S. K. Ghosh2, C. P. Suresh2, A. N. Dey1 and Gopal Shukla31Department of Forestry,2Pomology & Post Harvest Technology, Faculty of Horticulture, Uttar Banga Krishi Vishwavidyalaya, Pundibari 3 ICAR Research Complex for Eastern Region, Research Center, Plandu Ranchi, India

DISCLAIMER

This book is intended solely for informational purposes, aiming to shed light on the vital role the Kingdom of plants plays in sustaining life. The information presented herein, from the microscopic mosses to the towering trees, is offered as a means to enhance awareness and appreciation for the fundamental services plants provide—accounting for 80% of our daily sustenance and 98% of the oxygen we breathe.

The narratives within delve into the Plant kingdom's role as a repository for the Basic Life Supporting System (BLISS!), encompassing food, air, water, fertile soil, life-saving drugs, and the silent wisdom communicated akin to monks.

This book is not a substitute for professional advice, and the author assumes no responsibility for any consequences resulting from the information presented. Readers are encouraged to seek professional guidance for specific situations and to act responsibly in their interactions with the botanical world. Your engagement with this book signifies your understanding of its informational nature and the importance of fostering a deeper connection with the plant kingdom.

ABOUT THE AUTHORS

Dr. Manoj Sarkar is from the Indian Forest Service (retd.) and did his doctorate in Botany. He puts in about 30 years of service as a senior-level officers. His cadre was allotted to Tamil Nadu.

He loves Plants and Forests. He is a prolific writer on plants in scientific journals and also in daily newspapers. His books on botany and medicinal plants are published by the Tamil Nadu Govt and also by the Govt of India. The present book is part of a series on the author-niche 'Self-Mastery through the Kingdom of Plants' to create awareness, love, and care to protect the plant community and protect ourselves.

His other two books in the same series are:

1. "Self-Mastery & Enlightenment through the Kingdom of Plants"

2. "The Self Awakening through the Plants & Forests"

MAY WE ASK YOU A FAVOR?

At the outset, we want to give you a big thanks for reading this book. You could have chosen any other book, but you took ours, and we appreciate this. We hope you have at least a few actionable insights that will positively impact your daily life.

Can we ask for 30 seconds more of your time?

We'd love it if you could leave a review of the book. That will help us grow our readership by encouraging folks to take a chance on our books.

Keeping it straight - *reviews are the lifeblood of any author.*

It will take less than a minute of your time but will tremendously help us reach out to more people. **Kindly provide your review at the store you bought this book from.** And we'd love to see your review. Thanks for your support.

9 798327 352285